For Linda

best friend, colleague, partner,
confidant, spouse, and
soul mate

SCHOLASTIC

Teaching Comprehension
With Questioning Strategies
That Motivate Middle School Readers

Larry Lewin

New York • Toronto • London • Auckland • Sydney
Mexico City • New Delhi • Hong Kong • Buenos Aires

Teaching *Resources*

Cover design by Adana Jimenez
Cover photo by Getty Images (57422976)
Interior design by Edie Weinberg
ISBN-13 978-0545-05899-5
ISBN-10 0-545-05899-6
Photos on pages 25, 26, 35, 46, 50, 93, and 96 by Donald Gruener creative services
(www.donaldgruener.com)

12 11 10 9 8 7 6 5 4 3 2   40   10 11 12 13 14 15/0

Table of Contents

Acknowledgments

I'd like to thank the following teachers:

Tom Cantwell, Cal Young Middle School, Eugene, Oregon

Carole Carlson, Springfield Middle School, Springfield, Oregon

Evan Chandler, Cedar Ridge Middle School, Oregon Trail School District, Sandy, Oregon

Annie Cooper, Reynolds Middle School, Fairview, Oregon

Terry Kennedy, Twin Peaks School, Marana School District, Tucson, Arizona

Julie LaConte, Hoech Middle School, St. Louis, Missouri

Cody Loy, Cal Young Middle School, Eugene, Oregon

Amy Miller, Millennium Middle School, South Lyon, Michigan

Tyler Nice, Hamlin Middle School, Springfield, Oregon

Bart Pollard, Cottage Grove High School, Cottage Grove, Oregon

Emily Robbins, Reynolds Middle School, Fairview, Oregon

Angie Ruzicka, Cal Young Middle School, Eugene, Oregon

David Sousa, William M. Davies Career and Technical School, Lincoln, Rhode Island

Dorothy Syfert, Monroe Middle School, Eugene, Oregon

John Waldron, Paul W. Kutz Elementary School, Doylestown, Pennsylvania

Jeff Wyman, Roosevelt Middle School, Eugene, Oregon

Howard Yank, Curriculum Resource Coordinator, Vancouver School District, Vancouver, Washington

I'd also like to thank:

Isabel Beck, author of *Questioning the Author* (Scholastic, 2006) and numerous other books and articles on reading and vocabulary acquisition, for kindly reading Chapter 3 and giving me feedback.

Taffy Raphael, creator of QAR (Question-Answer Relationships) and author of *QAR Now* (Scholastic, 2006) and numerous books and articles, for kindly reading Chapter 3 and giving me feedback.

A. Vincent Ciardiello, author of *Puzzle Them First* (IRA, 2007) and numerous articles and lessons, for reading Chapter 2 and giving me feedback.

Sarah Longhi, senior editor at Scholastic Teaching Resources, for her support, encouragement, and determined editing. Without her, my manuscript never would have hatched into this book.

Wendy Mass, author of A *Mango-Shaped Space* for her permission to use her e-mail to students.

Putting Readers in the Driver's Seat

● Why doesn't the author just come out and tell us that?
~ Mitchell, a seventh-grade science student reading his textbook

During a lesson on how to generate questions while reading, a group of seventh graders was wrestling with a chapter in their science textbook on "The Nutritional Needs of Plants," and a particularly dense paragraph was causing some confusion. I led the students through a questioning strategy called Questioning the Author, or QtA (Beck & McKeown, 1997), which trains readers to be aware of the human being behind the words on the page. We discussed the possible intentions of the textbook's author, debating various interpretations of the words in the paragraph describing plant foods and absorption.

After the students had reached a consensus on the paragraph's meaning, one of the group members, Mitchell, said matter-of-factly, "Why doesn't the author just come out and tell us that?" He wasn't exasperated or frustrated in his question; he just sounded curious.

This was one of those instances of classroom enlightenment that we teachers yearn for—a genuine "aha" moment. Mitchell and the other kids in the group were realizing that reading is a two-way street, a partnership forged between them and the author. To comprehend text, they were discovering, the reader must work *with the author* to construct meaning. Mitchell understood that the author did the best he could, and now it was up to the reader to meet the writer halfway. This realization has a profound impact on students' comprehension because it changes their perception of what a reader is: not a passive recipient sitting back and waiting, but an active participant, engaged, in charge—a reader in the driver's seat.

From Punishment to Partnership

Too many of our middle-grade students view reading as a school assignment, something that is put upon them by their teachers. They may understand that the purpose of the reading is to "learn something" about math, social studies, art, literature, or health, but it is an exhausting event. The topics are not all that interesting to them, the words are too busy on the page, they may not possess enough prior knowledge on the topic to support comprehension, and they may lack the mental energy to tackle school reading. In short, for the legions of our below-grade-level readers, reading is a punishing enterprise. Something must change. We must figure out how to positively influence students' attitudes toward reading in order to convince them that reading is, in fact, a good thing.

Students Asking Questions of the Author

I have found that when students ask questions, they bring the author back into their reading. This opens students to a monumental realization: Reading is a communication between two people, a writer and a reader, with the purpose of exchanging important information about a topic. For example, consider these two questions from a sixth-grade reader to Witi Ihimaera, author of the novel *The Whale Rider*. This student is confused by the words of the author in an early chapter, and she is seeking clarification:

- Who is the narrator of this story?

- Why is our book different from the CD recording?

Or these questions to the author of a social studies textbook from an eighth grader receiving additional reading instruction from his school's learning support center:

- Why do you put a lot of non-necessary info in here?

- How is Lone Star Republic important?

Or these questions to the author of a science book about a chapter on geology:

- So if geologists studied seismic waves, why don't you say what it is or how it works?

- Will you explain the Earth's magnetic [fields] more simple?

Or this question directed at the author of a reading passage on bone health:

> ◉ Henry, are you saying that I'm creating my bones I'll need for the rest of my life?

These students have learned to rely on the author to help them learn what their teacher is trying to teach them. By asking the author these questions, they are showing their understanding that reading is an active communication between two people: the author and the reader.

While this view of reading-as-communication seems patently obvious to me—and the students in the foregoing examples—I have found this notion to be patently unobvious to most middle school students. Try it yourself: Ask your students to describe what reading is. If even one student mentions the word "communication" or "exchange" or "conversation" or "author," send me an e-mail, and I will nominate that kid for immediate induction into the Reading Hall of Fame.

By establishing the notion that reading is really accomplished through a partnership between author and reader, students gain a new attitude and a new purpose for reading. If they come to see that their job while reading is to figure out what the author wants them to know, reading becomes a quest, an expedition for understanding—and not some cruel teacher punishment. And this surely beats the standard, overused purpose of school reading: "To read the story and answer the questions," or "Read the chapter and outline it…".

This book is all about getting developing readers to shift their perception of reading as a punishment to reading as a partnership.

To achieve this goal, we must invite the authors of the reading materials we assign into our classrooms. Because this is physically difficult to pull off, we must teach our students how to mentally include the authors in their quest for comprehension. We will accomplish this by teaching them how to actively ask questions of the author as they read. This may not come easily to all students, but with the 11 new and engaging activities presented in this book, it will come.

Research That Lays the Foundation for This Book

Here are summaries of some of the research on which the strategies and activities in this book are based.

1. Transactional Theory of Reading

Transactional theory, advocated by Louise Rosenblatt, suggests a "reciprocal, mutually defining relationship" (1986) between the reader and the assigned text. Students are only part of the reading-comprehension equation. It is the transaction between the reader and the text that results in comprehension. Actually, a transaction between three: the reader, the author, and the text serving as the middle person.

R. E. Probst (1987) neatly summarizes the effect the Transactional Theory of Reading has on us:

> "A teacher who applies transactional theory will not view a literary experience as identical with the text from which it emerges. Rosenblatt argues for a redefinition of terms, suggesting that it is misleading to speak of the text as 'poem' (which will serve here as a general term for any [written work]). The text is simply ink on paper until a reader comes along. The 'poem', on the other hand, is what happens when the text is brought into the reader's mind and the words begin to function symbolically, evoking, in the transaction, images, emotions, and concepts. That symbolic functioning can happen only in the reader's mind. It does not take place on the page, in the text, but in the act of reading."

So whether we assign a story, a play, a poem, a textbook chapter, a Web resource, or whatever, the text is merely words on paper (or on a screen) until our student-readers come along to give it life inside their minds through the act of reading. As Probst writes, "The text in the absence of a reader is simply print . . . ." I like that.

2. Literary Criticism/Critical Reading

Literary criticism is an approach to reading in which the reader explains, analyzes, and/or evaluates the text. Clearly, this approach puts the reader in an active position. Far from being a passive recipient of the author's words, the reader assumes a role equal to that of the text.

According to 42explore.com, the educational Web site of Annette Lamb and Larry Johnson, "Literary criticism is a view or opinion on what a particular written work means. It is about the meanings that a reader finds in an author's literature. Literary criticism is an attempt to evaluate and understand the creative writing, the literature of an author. . . ." Because critiquing is higher on thinking hierarchies than comprehending, recalling, and retelling, I prefer it. Upper-level thinking is why I became a teacher in 1973 and why I continue to be in education.

3. Research on Reading Strategies

In the early-to-mid 1980s, reading researchers identified a set of reading comprehension strategies that skilled readers apply in order to problem-solve while reading. These researchers were inspired by a seminal article published by Dolores Durkin in 1978, in which she reported that "... fewer than 28 of 4,469 minutes *(less than 1%)* observed during reading periods in 24 fourth-grade classrooms in 13 districts were devoted to teaching students how to comprehend. Instead, the greatest portion of class time was devoted to assessment of comprehension where teacher questions dominated: Teachers assigned students to read and then asked them questions about what they read." Uh-oh. This was very shocking news, shocking enough that it helped launch a revolution in reading instruction. According to Ruth Yopp-Edwards, "This finding resulted in great attention to research in comprehension instruction over the next couple of decades—a time that has been referred to as the Golden Age of Comprehension because so much was learned about comprehension processes and the teaching of comprehension."

What emerged from researchers such as P. David Pearson, Dale D. Johnson, Isabel Beck, Taffy Raphael, and Robert J. Tierney was a set of reading comprehension strategies. Yopp-Edwards again: "Reading strategies that have been demonstrated to enhance comprehension include the following: monitoring comprehension, using graphic and semantic organizers, answering questions, *asking questions*, summarizing, using prior knowledge, and constructing mental images . . ." [italics mine]. The strategy of asking questions was identified and recommended; how to teach this strategy *to students* has been a major focus of my career—and it is the focus of this book.

4. The NAEP Reading Scores

The National Assessment of Educational Progress (NAEP), known as the Nation's Report Card, assesses student reading ability by asking questions that require upper-level thinking as opposed to mere recall. According to the "What Does the NAEP Reading Assessment Measure?" section of the NAEP Web site, students in grades 4, 8, and 12 are assessed on four different aspects of reading (see box).

1. **Forming a general understanding: The reader must consider the text as a whole and provide a global understanding of it.**

2. **Developing interpretation: The reader must extend initial impressions to develop a more complete understanding of what was read.**

3. **Making reader/text connections: The reader must connect information in the text with knowledge and experience.**

4. **Examining content and structure: This requires critically evaluating, comparing and contrasting, and understanding the effect of such features as irony, humor, and organization.**

You will see clearly that aspects 2, 3, and 4 require student readers to go far deeper than the first one. The good news for fourth graders nationally is that in 2007, "The percentages of students both at or above Basic and at or above Proficient rose five points compared with 1992. More specifically, over two-thirds (69%) of all fourth graders were measured at or above the Basic level, with one-third of them (33%) at or above the Proficient level, and 8 percent at the Advanced level."

However, the bad news is that only 8 percent of all fourth graders are at an Advanced level of reading comprehension, defined as ". . . being able to *generalize about topics* in the reading selection and demonstrate *an awareness of how authors compose* and use literary devices. When reading text appropriate to fourth grade, they should be able to *judge text critically* and, in general, to give thorough answers that indicate *careful thought.*" [Italics mine] In other words: to be able to read very well.

Eighth graders, too, improved their scores in 2007, with 74 percent at or above Basic [an increase], 31 percent at or above Proficient [no change], and 3 percent at or above Advanced, defined as ". . . being able to describe the *more abstract themes and ideas* of the overall text. When reading text appropriate to eighth grade, they should be able to *analyze both meaning and form and support their analyses explicitly* with examples from the text; they should be able to *extend text information* by relating it to their experiences and to world events. At this level, student responses should *be thorough, thoughtful, and extensive.*" [Italics mine] This reality is disconcerting: only 3 percent of all eighth graders in the U.S. can do this. We need to better. And we will.

5. *Puzzle Them First* by Vincent Ciardiello

You will see his name often in this book because Dr. Ciardiello has helped me greatly to think about ways to stimulate student question-asking—or in the words of his book's subtitle: "question-finding." He writes in his preface:

> ". . . I propose . . . that to truly learn something one must be bewildered or puzzled about new knowledge. It is my premise that there is strong educational value in creating cognitive confusion in students' minds so they are driven to ask challenging questions to offset the mental disequilibrium created by the puzzling situation" (2007).

Ciardiello advocates *intentionally* puzzling students by presenting them with a set of materials that "create cognitive confusion." My approach is slightly different: Instead of seeking materials designed to surprise, confuse, or confound students, I suggest that most of the reading we assign will provide moments of confusion as our student-readers engage with it. Reading typically has some bumps in the comprehension highway, and readers can be thrown off course by them—a phenomenon also known as "not getting it." This book provides you with a set of activities that enable students to *recognize* when they hit a bump and to *react* to it by asking a question that seeks to clarify understanding. Ciardiello writes of puzzlement and wonderment questions, and he offers very clear and helpful definitions of both. In Chapter 2, I offer my own take on how to encourage students to ask both of these types of questions

6. The Famous Questioning Frameworks

No book on student questioning could be complete without reference to the classic questioning frameworks of Questioning the Author (QtA) and Question-Answer Relationships (QAR). QtA was created by Isabel Beck, Margaret McKeown, and their associates in 1993. This approach to reading comprehension empowers students to question the author while seeking to understand his or her intended message. QtA helps students get over their subconscious belief in the infallibility of the author and recognize that sometimes authors produce writing that is not as good as it should be to support the transaction that needs to occur between reader and writer.

Likewise, QAR earns special treatment in this book because for decades it has enabled teachers to help their students learn how to seek answers through identifying different type of questions. You may already be using terms like "Right There," "Think & Search," and "Author and Me." If you are, you can thank Taffy Raphael and her colleagues Kathryn Au and Kathy Highfield (2006). I draw upon both approaches in this book, and I feature them in detail in Chapter 3.

How to Use This Book

Three years ago I wrote a book titled *Reading Response That Really Matters to Middle Schoolers* (2006) in which I advocated teaching our students how to "talk back" to the authors we assign them. I recommended a number of different writing formats for students to politely express their comments, analyses, and opinions of the assigned readings with the payoff of actually sending these student-to-author critiques to the author. Students' questions to the author were a key component of these "talk backs."

This new book, which serves as a companion to *Reading Response* because it redoubles my efforts to increase the depth of student questions, includes a collection of activities created to advance student question-asking with increasing complexity. Each chapter is designed to build upon and advance beyond the preceding chapter. However, this format is not a lockstep "scope and sequence" that requires a linear implementation. You can try the activities in the order they are presented, or you can extract them in any order you choose.

Chapter 1 introduces starter activities for student-generated questioning, which gently guide our readers to become question formulators. We begin with the Interview Your Teacher, where students interview us, their teachers, for practice. As a bridge, in the Chain Notes activity, the teacher asks the students a question. Next, students are introduced to the notion of a *hierarchy of questions*—the idea that some questions probe deeper than others. The last activity, Questions to the Teacher, introduces Puzzlement and Wonderment questions.

The activities in Chapter 2 invite the author back into the reading. All of these intermediate-level activities are designed to increase students' ability to mentally frame questions while reading in order to support active comprehension. We will consider a host of different types of questions, including ones that the teacher generates, those posed to an author, and literal versus more complex questions.

Chapter 3 gives you a quick tour of the classic Question-Answer Relationships and Questioning the Author. I will show you how I adjusted these powerful frameworks to bump up middle school students' ability to generate their own questions. Chapter 4 provides Advanced Questioning Activities, including questions adapted from Bloom's

Taxonomy. Additionally, this chapter includes an important section on the role of prior knowledge in questioning, which not only relates to the activities in this chapter but to all the preceding activities by reinforcing the critical role of background knowledge in question-asking.

Goals for This Book

My goal is to provide you with a full menu of question-asking activities so that you can select the ones you think will best connect to the learners in your classroom. These activities provide a cumulative effect: Each one strengthens the skill of questioning to create a snowballing affect toward competence. Our goal is for self-questioning while reading to become natural for students.

As you read the chapters, you will no doubt see some overlap among the activities, some repetition even. This is because each activity has much in common with the others. You will notice that some of the activities are somewhat similar, but have different labels to define them or different packaging to teach them. Whichever ones you pick, remember that the goal is to make it a normal occurrence for students to ask questions as they read.

Why bother? Question-asking improves reading in three important ways:

1. It fosters *self-monitoring* by helping the reader keep abreast of his or her progress on the road to understanding. When you are asking questions, you are tracking your reading.

2. It advances toward *close comprehension,* which is deeper and more careful than the kind of superficial comprehension gained by gliding over the text.

3. It cultivates *intellectual curiosity*—yes, real interest in learning—by lifting the veil of a book's words and inviting the reader to come inside. By questioning, you can consider the author's purpose, intention, position, attitude, or maybe even bias.

In short, self-questioning makes a reader a participant in the reading, no longer a bystander. So, our goal is to teach our students that by making a habit of asking questions, they can push their way past the words on the page and gain a deeper understanding of what they read.

CHAPTER 1

Starter Activities for Student-Generated Questioning

○ Are you a sports fan?

○ Are you for or against watching television, and do you loooovvve American Idol?

○ Why did you decide to become a teacher? Are you glad, or do you regret it?

~ Interview questions from students to their teacher

Because questioning has been identified as an essential strategy of reading comprehension (see "Research on Reading Strategies" on page 11), we need to develop lessons that will teach questioning strategies to our students who do not yet know how to create their own questions. This chapter offers you three starter activities to get the ball rolling.

You'll notice that the role of the author is not a part of these first activities. The following activities are meant to provide practice in question-asking, so at first, we the teachers will serve as an audience. We will bring the author into the equation in Chapter 2.

Interview Your Teacher

Student questioning is easily introduced by conducting a student-to-teacher oral interview in which we teach them how to ask questions—and they begin to see how their questions have differences. Of course, students already know how to ask their teachers questions; they do it constantly. But the vast majority of these questions are of the "Will it be on the test?" or "Can I have an extension?" variety. The type of questions I am advocating are those that clarify new information, seek more information, or probe meaning in another way. These more probing types of questions do not occur often enough in classrooms. And since they typically do not come naturally, they need to be taught.

We can introduce this form of questioning in a get-acquainted activity at the beginning of the school year or a new semester. Ask your students if they have any questions about you. The purpose is not only to break the ice and get acquainted, but also to introduce the idea of different levels of questions. As the four student-to-teacher questions quoted at the beginning of this chapter indicate, questions do come in different degrees of complexity.

I learned about this questioning activity from a friend and former colleague, Howard Yank, who taught high school social studies for many years and now works as the curriculum resource coordinator for the Vancouver School District in Washington state. Howard based the activity, which he called the "Public Interview," on a student activity described in Sidney Simon's *Values Clarification*. I modified this activity for middle-grade students, and I changed the name to "Interview Your Teacher."

A Teacher Gets Interviewed by His Sixth Graders

Evan Chandler teaches a sixth-grade language arts/social studies cluster class at Cedar Ridge Middle School in Sandy, Oregon, which includes ELL students, those on IEPs (Individualized Education Plan), students who lack support services, and some who perform at grade level. Here are some of the questions his students asked him in the interview:

- Do you like basketball?

- What movie do you hate the most?

- If you had one chance to be a celebrity for a day, who would you be?

- What is the weirdest dream you've ever had?

- Have you seen any of the "Scary Movies"?

- Would you rather fly or be invisible?

- What did you think about the soccer World Cup?

The student questions need to be recorded—written on the board, an overhead transparency, or typed into your computer connected to a projector so everyone can see them. Alternatively, you can deputize a student to act as the scribe to write questions down for the class to be photocopied later. Next, to transition from getting acquainted with the teacher to analyzing the questions for the degree of complexity, students are asked to simply sort the questions into two categories. I like to keep the directions minimal because this strategy fosters inductive, not deductive, thinking, rather than guiding students toward predetermined categories.

The sorting can be done in a whole-class setting with the teacher leading the discussion; alternatively students can be put into pairs, trios, or groups of four, or they can do the task individually. The choice of configuration is based on the teacher's perception of the students' ability to tackle this task. For all options, Howard suggests providing students with index cards or separate pieces of paper for sorting the questions.

Evan decided to use the small-group method. He discovered that the majority of the groups were sorting questions based on content (movies, sports, career, etc.). Okay, that's good, but one group sorted questions by their first words (who, what, when, etc.). Interesting.

In the next step, Evan conducted a whole-class conversation on the groups' categories, and found that the two major categories were questions with simple answers and questions that required a more elaborate answer. Class discussion is a key ingredient to teaching students how to ask and categorize questions. Ciardiello refers to it as "engaging in critical conversations"(2007).

Evan reports, "In our class discussion, we noted how many questions were answerable with a simple *yes* or *no* (16/50). Because there were so many, they could be seen as a subcategory of the basic questions, which we defined as 'requiring only one or two words in response.'"

The number of categories and the characteristics of those categories matter less than the *thinking* required in determining them. To me, there are no "right" or "wrong" categories; rather, it is the *conversation* that reveals how students came up with the categories that we're after. Remember, our second goal in this activity is to get kids to begin to think about a hierarchy of questions.

Evan's students greatly enjoyed the opportunity to ask him questions. "We ended up spending an entire period (45 minutes) introducing the activity and conducting the interview. I allowed them to continue the interview until I sensed that they had exhausted their ability to find creative questions."

Thoughts for Next Time

Evan later realized that during the interview he had inadvertently provided extra information in answering some student questions. He sometimes elaborated in response to simple questions, and he occasionally found himself prompting his students.

"As the students asked questions, I frequently volunteered more information than their questions required. I often offered an explanation in response to a yes-or-no question, but I would (and am planning to) respond differently next time. I guided my students by asking questions like, 'Do you want to know if I've seen this movie, or do you want to know what I think about it?' "

Evan decided that in the future, his answers would only go into as much detail as the question required, thus encouraging students to think carefully about what information they are actually hoping to receive from him.

Also, as a follow-up, Evan considered inviting a guest to the class, perhaps an administrator or school counselor, as the second interviewee.

Here is the recommended procedure for the Interview Your Teacher Activity

1. Tell students they are going to interview you. Explain Howard Yank's three rules of a Public Interview: 1) If I answer a question, it has to be an honest answer. 2) If for any reason I don't want to answer a question, I will simply say, "I pass." No need to explain. 3) At the end of the interview, I can ask a question back to the interviewer that I answered earlier.

2. If the class seems outgoing and comfortable, students can submit their questions orally during discussion. Alternatively, if they are more reserved, you can tell them to write down their questions on scratch paper (or supplied index cards) and turn them in. Then you can select which questions you want to read and answer for the whole class.

3. If students are unsure how to proceed, prime the pump by asking yourself a question, or better yet, a few questions. First, model a basic type of question like "How long have I taught at this school?" and then a deeper type of question like "Which course is my favorite to teach and why?"

4. As you receive the questions, record them (in an abbreviated version if necessary) on the board, overhead, or computer. The recording is essential because you and the students will later be reviewing the questions to categorize them into levels. I suggest deputizing a student who is a quick writer to neatly transcribe all the questions on paper, so that they can be photocopied and then cut into individual slips for categorization.

5. Periodically pause and refer to the listed questions. Ask students if they notice a trend in the different types of questions being asked. The goal is for them to begin to identify a simple, basic question as opposed to a deeper, more advanced question.

6. The number of questions you receive depends on your students' level of interest in this activity and whether some of the questions are of the deeper, more advanced type. You decide how long to continue.

7. Print up the question list, refer to it on the board or screen, or better yet, provide questions printed on slips of paper or on cards. Make sure the questions are numbered, and tell the students to sort them into categories on a sheet of paper. I like to give them a few minutes to consider this independently.

8. Group students into pairs, trios, or quads, and tell them to share their groupings to see if they agree or disagree. Tell them they can change the categories if a group member convinces them.

9. Debrief as a whole class by discussing the categories:
   - What is a good name for each category?
   - What is a good definition for each category?
   - How many categories do we have?
   - Which questions belong in each category? Why?

10. Summarize the purpose of this interview activity by telling the class that different types of questions will be important in this course, and that they will be working with question types periodically.

Different Interviews in Different Classrooms

As with all the questioning activities you will learn in this book, the teacher interview can be modified and adapted in many ways. Here are three adaptations.

1. Students Interview Students

Annie Cooper modified this activity a bit for her students at Reynolds Middle School in Fairview, Oregon, to make sure all of them would be involved. Before asking teacher questions, they conducted student-to-student interviews by writing down 10 questions for a classmate. Annie gave them the rules for the questions (see Step #1 on page 19), then wrote the questions on the whiteboard for everyone to see. Finally, she led a discussion on how the class could put them into categories. Annie was pleasantly surprised to find that all of her kids took part and were engaged by the activity.

2. Student Self Survey

Amy Miller, an intervention module teacher at Millennium Middle School in South Lyon, Michigan, made an adjustment for her smaller classes with five or so support students who do not qualify for special ed. Instead of partnering them, she had each of them take a survey about themselves (see page 22), which introduced self-questioning.

Notice that at the end of the survey, Amy asks students to write down two questions for her. Amy reported that the activity engaged the students. "They were on-task," she said. And they were learning about question types.

3. Playing the "Getting to Know You" Game

Carole Carlson, of Springfield, Oregon, went from teaching high school to middle school students this year, and found a way to integrate student questioning into her "Getting to Know You" activity with her eighth graders. She explains: "In 'Getting to Know You,' students have to tell three interesting but appropriate facts about themselves. Then, we play Name Bingo using those facts. Students have to listen carefully to remember the information about their new classmates."

Student Survey

What is your full name? _____

Do you prefer to be called by another name? If so, what is it? _____

List any sports, clubs, groups, activities, hobbies, etc., that you participate in (in school and out of school). _____
_____

Do you have any pets? If so, what kind? _____

Do you have any brothers or sisters? If so, what are their names and ages? _____
_____
_____

Do you have a computer at home? _____ Do you have Internet access? _____

What do you want to do after high school? What do you want to do after college? _____
_____
_____

If you could change one thing in this world, what would it be? _____
_____
_____

What do you think is the biggest problem middle school students face? _____
_____
_____

What do you think is the biggest problem middle school teachers face? _____
_____
_____

If you could travel anywhere in the world, where would you go? _____
_____
_____

FAVORITES

School Subject _____   Friend _____

Singer/Band _____   Teacher _____

Book/Series _____   Sports Team _____

TV Show _____   Animal _____

Movie _____   Activity _____

What else would you like to tell me? _____
_____
_____

What are two questions that you would like to ask me? _____
_____
_____

Source: Amy Miller, Millennium School, South Lyon, Michigan

"After the Bingo activity they got to interview me. As the students gave info and asked questions, we used the 'Thin and Thick' technique (see page 54) for sorting them. My eighth-grade students then interviewed their classmates for the school newspaper. Good idea to start using key higher thinking skills from the get-go." Carole makes a good point: Using questioning activities right away boosts higher-level thinking. Nod your head if you like the idea of your students thinking at a higher level!

Chain Notes

I learned this activity from the Web site of the National Teaching and Learning Forum (http://www.ntlf.com/html/lib/bib/assess.htm). Utilizing the concept of a chain letter, Chain Notes provide a quick assessment to ensure that all students can respond to a teacher query. I like to use it to introduce question-asking (see box on page 24).

Ancient China Chain Notes Questions

First period in Tyler Nice's sixth-grade World History class at Hamlin Middle School in Springfield, Oregon, is a challenge. Due to the school's scheduling gods, Tyler has lots of ESL students and quite few kids with Individualized Education Plans (IEPs). The challenge is to help all his students learn the important social studies content. To do this, Tyler uses a variety of instructional strategies, including hands-on activities, videotapes/DVDs, mini-lectures/discussion, and of course, reading in the textbook.

The chapter called "The Legacy of Ancient China" in McDougal Littell's *World History Ancient Civilizations* (2006) is well written and interesting. However, it looked like a potentially tough read for some students, so I suggested to Tyler that we modify the Chain Notes activity to assist his students' comprehension. Instead of one shared envelope with a single question written on the back as suggested on page 24, each student was given a small unsealed envelope with *two* question cards inside (see Figure 1.1).

The instructions we gave to the students were: "Open your envelope and read both question cards before beginning the chapter. Then read the first page of the chapter carefully and answer both questions on a piece of paper. When you finish, fold and insert your answer paper—with your name, date, and class period on top—into the envelope, along with the two question cards, and 'mail' it back to your teacher."

In the envelopes were:

- a question on pink paper that addressed a *confusing place* in the chapter

- a question on green paper that addressed a *curious place* in the chapter

Chain Notes Implementation Procedure

1. On the front of a large envelope write your name and address, and on the back write a question about the topic the class is reading.

2. Hand the envelope to a student and have him or her respond to the question by writing a short answer on a piece of scratch paper and placing it in the envelope. (Providing students with uniform pieces of scratch paper might be helpful.)

3. Instruct the student to pass the envelope to the next student, who reads your question on the outside, thinks about an answer, writes it on a separate piece of scratch paper, and then inserts it into the envelope.

4. The procedure continues until all students have responded. This activity may take the entire period, only part of a period, or perhaps several periods.*

5. When the last student has responded, collect the envelope. After class, go through the student responses to determine the best criteria for categorizing their answers with the goal of detecting response patterns. You could cluster their answers by:
   - correct versus incorrect
   - brief versus thorough
   - least to most complex
   - basic factual answers to those that go beyond the book
   - other

6. The next day, debrief with students the patterns of responses you identified by explaining the categories of answers you determined and sharing some examples. This process serves to model to students the notion of *degree*, which will play a major role in forthcoming activities.

* Of course, while the envelope is making its way around the classroom, students are not sitting around waiting for it to arrive at their desks. This would be a waste of instructional time. Rather, this activity occurs simultaneously with another assignment, so that all students are working throughout the entire period. Instruct them not to sit and wait.

A "confusing place," we told the class, is when the author provided information in the chapter that we were supposed to understand, but we did not.

A "curious place" is when the author does not give us enough information about something we would like to know more about.

Here are the teacher-modeled questions Tyler and I developed for just the first page of the chapter. Each student received one of each in the envelope:

Pink   Why was silk a "much desired luxury product"?

Pink   Why were horses "especially valued" more than the other goods?

Green   I wonder if the Chinese people liked the new ideas and customs or if they preferred their own.

Green   I wonder if it was dangerous traveling on the Silk Road trail.

The Chain Notes questions from the teacher to the students serve three purposes: 1. To establish a purpose for reading, i.e., read carefully to find answers to the teacher's questions, 2. To model a useful reading comprehension strategy, i.e., question asking, and 3. To provide the teacher with a quick assessment of understanding (or misunderstanding).

Figure 1.1 Receiving an envelope from their teacher with questions piqued students' curiosity.

Student Answers to Chain Notes Questions

As Tyler's sixth graders read the chapter's first page, they answered their pink and green questions on scratch paper (see Figure 1.2).

Here are some of the students' answers to the pink question, "Why was silk a 'much desired luxury product?' "

- Silk is desired because it's fancy and soft

- Because it was light and was fancy

- Because it's expensive

Figure 1.2 Sixth graders write Chain Notes answers on scratch paper.

- To stay cool

- People want silk because that's the best kind of clothes they can get.

Okay, very good, these kids are understanding the idea. Some students provided more elaborate answers:

- Because so many people wanted the silk and they traded it. Silk was used for clothes often times. It was much desired as a luxury fabric by both Chines [Chinese] and people outside of China. Chines silk was important.

- Silk was much desired in China because of it's a luxury

product because it is beautiful and long lasting and you can dye it brilliant. You could make clothes out of it and they got traded for gold and silver out of the other lands since they did not have that kind of mineral.

This last answer included some words copied from the text without using quotation marks. This is bound to happen, so it makes sense to tell your students that they can use some words from the book, but to enclose them in quotation marks to show that you are borrowing, not stealing.

This answer shows some confusion:

- Yes, because you can write on them.

My approach to remedying this kind of misunderstanding is to pose the question to the whole class the next day. I would describe silk, or even have a sample in hand and ask if silk was used as paper to write on. I would underscore how silk was used without identifying the student with the misunderstanding. Later, I would double back to that student to ensure that he or she had an accurate understanding.

Here are some answers that Tyler received for the green (curious) question, "I wonder if it was dangerous traveling on the Silk Road trail."

- It was dangerous because people could die on the way there if they don't have food.

- Yes, it was because you could get murdered or ramsact [ransacked] by people.

The next answers employ useful starter words like "I think" and "Probably":

- I think it was because if you ran out of water on the way you would die of thirst.

- Probably what's dangerous about traveling on the trail is rivers, rocky areas, and thieves.

Tyler received the following answers to the deeper green question, "I wonder if the Chinese people liked the new ideas and customs or if they preferred their own."

- People of China *probably* liked the new ideas and customs better than their own because they learned and were curio [Spanish word for *curious*].

⦾ *I think* they liked the new ideas because now that they have silk they can make rich clothes.

The following answer shows the seed of a good idea, but it needs more elaboration:

⦾ Better—because *evolving*

And these answers definitely need elaboration:

⦾ Yeah, I think so.

⦾ Probably did

⦾ Ya, because their [they're] different

Assessing Reading Comprehension

The third purpose of Chain Notes, to provide a quick assessment of comprehension, is very helpful to a social studies teacher who obviously needs to know how well his students are understanding the content he is teaching. Chain Notes provide a formative assessment as the unit progresses, which is far more useful than a traditional unit test given at the end of the term (summative assessment), when it may be too late.

You will notice that the students' answers relied on some *speculation*: The students had to make some kind of leap from reading the literal text to coming up with an answer of their own because the text either assumed they had an understanding of the subject matter or it skipped over some points. In either case, answering the question requires students to interpret, to make inferences, by filling in the missing information.

Although some students were better able to do this than others, this is still a useful whole-class activity. I am convinced that without asking these questions, many middle-grade readers would not be able to monitor their understanding as they read.

Questions Mailed to My Teacher

This next activity teaches young readers how to generate their own questions while reading and provides a mini-assessment of gaps in students' comprehension. While similar to Chain Notes, it has important differences:

- There is no teacher question on the back or inside the envelope. Instead, each student asks the teacher a question.

- Their questions are based on the reading assignment instead of a teacher interview.

Questions Mailed to My Teacher Procedure

1. Pass around a large unsealed envelope addressed to you with a tablet of blank scratch paper inside. If you've done the Chain Notes activity, ask your students if anyone recognizes the envelope and can review for the class the procedure from last time. Someone should remember the procedure for Chain Notes; if not, review the procedure with them.

2. Tell them that this new activity is similar to Chain Notes, but different in two key ways (see above).

3. Show them the tablet of scratch paper inside the envelope. Tell them: "When the envelope arrives at your desk, open it, remove the tablet, tear off a piece of paper, write a question about the reading assignment along with your answer, and then slip it back inside." (To speed up this activity, the teacher could distribute the scratch paper to each student, have them write down their questions, and when the envelope arrives, put the question inside and pass the envelope to the next student.) Be sure students understand that the envelope should remain unsealed.

4. Once you receive the envelope back, read over the questions to determine the degree of questioning your class is generating. You could sort into "confused" and "curious" questions as suggested for Chain Notes (see page 25), or you could consider Puzzlement versus Wonderment questions, which are described in detail in our next section.

"Puzzlement and Wonderment" Questions to My Teacher

In Tyler Nice's sixth-grade World History class, we did a variation on the color-coded Chain Notes type of questions, but this time the students had to make up their own questions and send them to the teacher. We used the same format of pink and green questions:

- **Pink** questions are about a *confusing place* in the chapter: The author thinks I get it, but I really don't.

- **Green** questions address a *curious place* in the chapter. The author mentions something I'd like to learn more about.

We renamed them puzzlement and wonderment questions, borrowing these terms from Ciardiello (see box).

Puzzlement and Wonderment Questions

My definitions are somewhat different from Ciardiello's originals:

- *Puzzlement questions* are those that arise when a reader encounters questions that cause confusion, bafflement, or uncertainty due to surprising information in the reading.

- Wonderment questions demonstrate "surprise and wonder," a desire for more information, a pondering of possibilities, an extension beyond the basic facts of the reading. They reveal a metacognitive awareness of the need to *seek additional information* to plug the gap.

I like teaching young readers different types of questions and how to generate them. Let's examine some.

Student Puzzlement Questions

Tim, a sixth grader, wrote the following puzzlement questions "to clear up the confusion" he felt as he read about the Egyptian pyramids in his social studies text:

- Why did grave robbers sometimes steal the mummy?

- Why are step pyramids called step pyramids?

Both of Tim's questions indicate that he is confused about various terms mentioned in the text and doesn't get what the author is trying to convey. Disappointing, for sure, but it is far better for him and his teacher that his teacher be aware of this than to assume Tim is getting it.

Puzzlement questions could begin, of course, with "I am puzzled by..." but here are some more puzzlement prompts that I have found useful:

- Am I *surprised* by anything in this reading?

- Is there anything *unusual* about the events/ideas in this reading?

- Did the author tell me something that I *didn't expect*?

- Is anything in this reading *different* from what I thought?

- Did the author write anything that was *contrary* to my expectations?

- And my current favorite because it's in kid language: *What's up* with _____ ?

This last question starter evolved during a conversation with Janelle, a sixth grader who had already written her two wonderment questions but was stuck on making up two Puzzlements. I reviewed some of the above prompts, but when I said to her, "It's like *What's up with that*?" she got it, because it pointed out a mismatch between what she thought and what the book said.

Student Wonderment Questions

Sixth grader Tim wrote the following wonderment questions in connection with the chapter on Ancient Egypt:

- I wonder why the people blamed the pharaohs for angering the gods.

- I wonder why the black curly thing [in the picture] is on the top of the crown of Lower Egypt.

How encouraging that a sixth grader is interested enough in the history of Ancient Egypt to request more information. For the teacher, this is useful feedback for deciding on where to go and what to do next in the unit.

Ciardiello offers a set of additional ways that students can begin their questions:

- What are some other ways . . . ?

- What if . . . ?

- Can you imagine . . . ?

- Can you suppose . . . ?

- Can you predict . . . ?

- If . . . then . . . ?

- How might . . . ?

A student's question, "What if there was no silk?" gets to a critical point in the chapter. If China had not produced silk, what would the impact have been on its trading relationship with other countries? This one really shows a desire to explore other possibilities.

Another question, "What is another way to explain Daoism?" seems to be asking for a better definition for this term.

In most of the following wonderment questions from Tyler's other students, kids started with *I wonder*, but notice the last two begin with *Why* and *How might*:

- **Gabriela:** I wonder if they still use Buddhism today?

- **Isaac:** I wonder what life was like for farmers before the inventions.

- **Isaac:** I wonder why Daoism is used mostly for Chinese.

- **Kendrick's:** I wonder [if] the inventions made the farmers LAZY.

- **Bianca's:** I wonder how many Dynastys [Dynasties] were there.

- **Nick:** I wonder why Daoism lasted longer than Confucianism.

- **Diana:** Why did Buddhism spread around so much?

- **Talysha:** How might the Chinese people protect the pottery [on the trading trail]?"

All of these wonderment questions indicate students' desire for more information than the text provided. These questions are a way to help our students:

- realize no single text can be the complete resource on a topic

- indicate opportunities for finding resources that go beyond the text

- launch deeper discussions about the topic

Any social studies teacher can appreciate the benefit of these outcomes. In fact, any teacher of any subject where reading is assigned can use puzzlement and wonderment questions to both support and assess reading comprehension.

Puzzlement Questions and the Role of Prior Knowledge

A teacher could modify this activity by bringing in the author of the reading assignment. In the following example, a sixth grader in Carole Carlson's class in Springfield Middle School in Springfield, Oregon, recognized a discrepancy between a reference to CAT scans in the book *Secrets of the Mummies* (1999) and her understanding of them.

- The confusing part of the book was when *she* [the author] was talking about how she was putting the mummy in the cat scan. I don't understand how the cat scan would work if the mummy was dead.

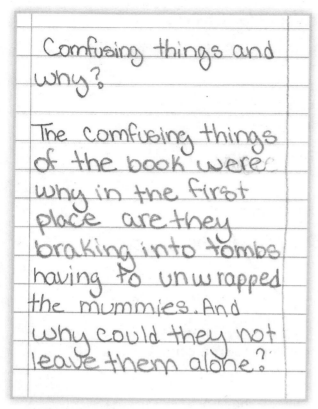

Figure 1.3 Zulema's puzzlement questions

Handwritten text in figure:
Comfusing things and why?

The comfusing things of the book were why in the first place are they braking into tombs having to unwrapped the mummies. And why could they not leave them alone?

This is a puzzlement question because the new information she encountered was not what she expected. She apparently believes that CAT scans are only given to live humans, not very dead ones. And by referring to the author in her questions, she is advancing her comprehension by this link.

Here are two puzzlement questions written by a student named Zulema (see Figure 1.3).

While she does not mention the author as the source of the puzzlement, she is aware that none of this information jibed with what she already knew, or *thought* she knew, about archeologists in Egypt. This *cognitive dissonance* is also an opportunity for learning.

In both examples, the student-reader is practicing metacognitive thinking by self-monitoring comprehension. When I asked Carole why her students were so able to recognize their comprehension gaps and generate puzzlement questions, she answered quickly and surely, "Because they know a lot about mummies." Turns out, the key to asking this type of question is possessing what Jeff Wilhelm calls "requisite schematic knowledge." Or as Vincent Ciardiello puts it in an e-mail message, "Without having at least some background knowledge on a topic, the student will not be able to reach a state of cognitive confusion which is the precursor to the generation of both types of questions. . . ."

A few of Carole's kids experienced some confusion due to a lack of prior knowledge, such as in the following example:

- **The confusing parts was the word embalming, and the names of the people was confusing, and then how they took out the brain.**

This kid is lacking a vocabulary term, ancient Egyptian names, and some knowledge of an archeological procedure. Not her fault, of course, but important that she recognized what was unclear to her. Later, in Chapter 4, we will consider a number of ways to boost requisite background knowledge.

Teaching Tips for Questions Mailed to My Teacher

Here are six tips for ensuring that this activity supports student questioning.

1. Provide Choice

You might give students a choice about which of the two question types they want to ask you. Or maybe you require three questions, but offer them the choice of type. You could also have everyone write a puzzlement question the first time you try this activity and a wonderment question the next time. Feel your way into this. To experiment with the different options, consider trying them in different classes. For example, your sluggish first-period class might be best served with everyone writing a wonderment question, but your third-period go-getters might benefit from being given the choice.

Figure 1.4 Students' color-coded questions

2. Form Groups to Clarify Questions

You could also add an intermediary stage between the question-writing and the delivery of questions to you. Put the students in pairs, trios, or groups of four, and let them read their questions to one other. The goal is for students to see if they agree on the question type before submitting them to you.

3. Color-Code Questions

Another way to help structure this questioning activity is for students to categorize question types using colored sticky notes. The color-coding enhances the activity by underscoring different of types of questions. The role of color in categorizing is obvious, as is the students' attraction to sticky notes.

You might first model the two color-categories using the overhead projector with colored pens, or alternatively, create colored sticky note shapes on the computer and project them onto the white screen for whole-class viewing. While modeling the two different types of questions, be sure to think aloud—talk about what you are thinking as you create puzzlement and wonderment questions for the overhead or computer.

Additionally, you can require that students generate a certain number of each type of question by distributing the same number of colored sticky notes. If you think three of each is sufficient, then give each kid three of each color. Tyler and I opted for two of each when we introduced the question types to his sixth graders (see Figure 1.4).

4. Assess Student Questions with a *ChecBric*

You'll need to decide whether you want your students to post their sticky note questions in the book, on their desk, or on a piece of notebook paper. Also decide if you want questions labeled with names or initials. Initials work best if you decide you want questions turned in to you, so that you can check them over. And if you decide you want to assess their questions, you might also consider using a two-columned scoring device known as a ChecBric (Lewin, 2006), meaning a combination checklist/rubric. Students use the left side to self-check their work, and you use the right side to circle the appropriate score (see page 37).

Puzzlement/Wonderment
Questions *ChecBric*

Student Checklist	Teacher Rubric
1. On my own, I could not ask a puzzlement or wonderment question about the reading, but with help: ⊙ I asked about a confusing fact in the reading. ⊙ I asked about a confusing important stated key detail ⊙ I asked about the deeper, more complicated important ideas not found in the reading	**SCORE 1** With help, the student is able to generate a puzzlement question(s) about basic recall/literal elements and a wonderment question, about some of the more complex, complicated unstated elements, a desire for more information, a pondering of possibilities, or an extension beyond the basic facts of the reading.
2. On my own, I was not able to ask a more complicated wonderment question, but I could ask a puzzlement question about the basic information that was in the reading: ⊙ I asked about a confusing fact in the reading ⊙ I asked about a confusing important stated key detail	**SCORE 2** Student independently generates a puzzlement question(s) regarding the basic recall/literal level key components.
3. On my own, I could ask questions about both the stated information, plus the more complicated questions: ⊙ I asked a puzzlement question(s) about a confusing fact or key detail **PLUS** ⊙ I was able to dig deeper and ask a more complicated wonderment question(s) that the author did not directly state in the reading	**SCORE 3** Student independently generates the puzzlement literal/recall questions and the more complicated wonderment inferential /between the lines questions that were explicitly taught with no major errors or omissions.
4. On my own, I could do all of 3, plus I also was able to go beyond what was taught because: ⊙ I asked a question that required an opinion about the information in the reading ⊙ I asked a question that required an evaluation about the information in the reading ⊙ I asked a question right to the author about a decision she/he made in the writing	**SCORE 4** In addition to a 3 performance, student independently exceeds what was taught by generating a question(s) that requires an opinion, an evaluation, or a challenge to the author.

Based on Scoring Scale by Robert Marzano in *Classroom Assessment & Grading That Works* (2006); ChecBric © 2008 Larry Lewin Educ. Consulting. larry@larrylewin.com 541•343•1577

How to Debug the Puzzlement and Wonderment Question Activity

Here are suggested solutions to some of the common problems that arise when students are learning to generate these types of questions.

PROBLEM #1. YOUR STUDENT CAN'T DO PUZZLEMENTS

It's possible that the student finds nothing unclear about the reading assignment and thus cannot come up with a puzzlement question.

Solution: Accept it as okay, because no puzzlement questions are needed, or consider asking the student a factual question about the assignment to test his or her understanding. If the student has trouble answering, you can say, "Hey, you can use it as your puzzlement question."

PROBLEM #2. YOUR STUDENT ASKS "FAKE" QUESTIONS

Some students short-circuit the learning process by making up a question that neither puzzles them nor causes them to wonder. Instead, they extract a few words from the text and plug in a question starter like, "I wonder what paper is?" While this can be frustrating to a teacher, it's important to view this behavior as a possible indication that the reader is truly struggling to comprehend the text. At the least, it shows that the student has very limited motivation to complete the reading assignment, which is a concern in itself.

Solution: Meet with the student, perhaps as part of a temporary grouping of several students, and reteach the concept of puzzlement questions. Show once again how you generate puzzlements and work through a paragraph or two together to see if they can identify puzzlement questions of their own. I would postpone wonderments for another day.

PROBLEM #3. YOU CAN'T TELL WHETHER THE QUESTIONS ARE FAKE OR SINCERE

Students often ask legitimate questions, like "I don't know what Daoism is" or "What is Buddhism?" that are answered later in the text.

Solution: I conduct a mini-lesson on the reading strategy of context clues and model for the kids how to orally pose a question, mentally save it, and carefully read on searching for an answer. (They can also jot it down and later erase or discard it.) Remind students that authors often take awhile before they supply needed information.

PROBLEM #4. YOUR STUDENT ASKS ANSWERABLE QUESTIONS

A student in Tyler's social studies class asked, "How did the wheel barrow make it easier for farmers to move heavy loads by hand?" Another asked, "Why did inventions make life easier for farmers?" Now, I would assume that a sixth grader would be able to comprehend how new agricultural inventions reduced work or freed up time, but it's possible he really didn't know, or perhaps he didn't really understand what "agricultural inventions" are. In fact, one student wrote, "What is agriculture?"

Solution: Meet with the student or a group, have them read their question(s), and ask if they can attempt to answer them. If so, great; if not, you refer to the text or if necessary, provide key background information. By discussing their questions and answers with you, the degree of authenticity versus fakeness will emerge. In my view, these students probably just need another shot at this task, with some closer teacher attention.

PROBLEM #5. YOUR STUDENT CONFUSES THE TWO TYPES OF QUESTIONS

Solutions Reteach the definitions and review the examples, or give new examples that you have intentionally mislabeled and see if anyone notices. If not, you can draw their attention to the mislabelled definition. You can also try using different labels like QAR's "Right There," "Think & Search," and "On My Own." But overall, don't worry too much about the categories. If a reader calls a question a puzzlement when it's actually more of a wonderment, no harm is done. What's really important, here and in all the activities in this book, is the act of questioning. By questioning, students are thinking about what they are reading, and that is what we are after. If they misunderstand a particular question category, so be it.

PROBLEM #6. YOUR STUDENT CAN'T ASK ANY QUESTIONS BECAUSE THE TEXT IS TOO TOUGH

If reteaching and using different labels for the categories does not help, it might be that the book is simply too far above their reading level. Uh-oh. Big problem: textbooks and students who cannot read them.

Solutions: Three solutions come to mind:

1. Have students listen to an audio version of the assignment, via CD player or iPod and have them read along softly as they listen. This is kind of intervention still works.

2. Use a paired reading activity called WRAP: Whisper Read Alternating Paragraphs. I learned this technique from a teacher named Tom Cantwell, and it works like this: Pair up two readers of similar ability. One reader goes first to whisper-read the first paragraph (or several). At the end, the listening partner makes a summarizing statement, the reader agrees or suggests a better one, and the roles reverse. With puzzlement and wonderment questions, partners can work together to come up with the required number.

3. Bail on the book and find a new one better suited to your students' skill level. Try using Lexile Levels, a useful online scale for rating the difficulty of a text. (http://www.lexile.com/DesktopDefault.aspx?view=ed&tabindex=6&tabid=18#1)

PROBLEM #7. THE ENVELOPE IDEA FOR MAILING TO THE TEACHER IS A HASSLE

Solution: Don't use envelopes or colored slips of paper. Tell your students to write their questions on notebook paper divided into two columns for the two types, or to write one type on the front of their paper and the other on the back. You will not be arrested by the Instructional Police for skipping the envelope idea.

5. Have Students Attempt to Answer Their Own Questions

You can modify the Questions Mailed to My Teacher activity by asking students to answer their own questions. Their answers may provide you with valuable insight into how well they are comprehending what they read.

6. Assign Question-Asking for Homework

What if students are better able to generate questions at home than in class? According to Marlene Scardamalia and Carl Bereiter (1992), middle school students who asked very few questions during a science-class discussion asked higher-level questions on the same subject when it was part of a homework assignment.

If you want to assign this as homework, consider using the following directions to provide motivation:

> "For homework tonight you are going to write down five questions about
> _____ [our topic]. You have a choice: You can write puzzlement questions
> worth two points each, or you can write wonderment questions worth up
> to three points each. Or, you can do a combination of both. It's your choice.
> The assignment is worth 10 points total, so you can see that by asking some
> wonderment questions you can earn a few extra credit points." See the box
> below for a list of Question Starters that might help get you going.

Puzzlement	Wonderment
I am puzzled by...	I wonder why...
I don't get why...	What are some other ways...
I am surprised by...	Can you imagine...
Why does it say...	Can you suppose...
I am confused by...	Can you predict...
This doesn't seem right...	What if...
How come...	If... then...
This is different than I...	How might...
I didn't expect ...	

Summary

Interview Your Teacher, Chain Notes, and Questions Mailed to My Teacher are basic introductory activities designed to gently guide students into question-asking. All three activities can be augmented with puzzlement and wonderment questions. Once students get used to asking questions during reading, they begin to realize that not all questions are created equal. Now is the time to move on to the next level.

CHAPTER 2

Intermediate Questioning Activities

- *What does DNA stand for?*
- *I wonder why each nucleotide consists of three different types of materials?*

~ Audrey's questions while reading about genetics in her science textbook.

Audrey's teacher, Annie Cooper, is worried about teaching science to her eighth graders at Reynolds Middle School in Fairview, Oregon. Well, worried may be too strong a word. Let's say that she is concerned for her below-grade-level readers whom she expects to have difficulty comprehending the course textbook. Anyone else have similar concerns about struggling readers making it through a textbook?

The state of reading in the U.S. is something to be concerned about. Based on the most recent NAEP reading scores of 2007, I believe we are facing a literacy crisis in this country. As stated in the Introduction, 33 percent of fourth graders tested at or above the Proficient level, and 8 percent at the Advanced level. At eighth grade, 31 percent were at Proficient and only 3 percent at Advanced (see NAEP Scores, page 11–12).

In Chapter 1, you read how the teacher can get the ball rolling in the right direction for students by showing them easy ways to start generating questions. This chapter provides teachers with a set of four proactive intermediate-level questioning activities designed to help all students tackle the reading assignments we give them by becoming alert instead of passive readers.

Teacher Modeling With Adult Text

In order to get your students to view reading not as a chore but as a pleasurable way of learning about new ideas, they must be active thinkers. This first activity is similar to the Chain Notes activity in Chapter 1, but this time the teacher asks questions about something unrelated to school, instead of a school assignment.

Share the Road License Plate Debuts in Oregon

Proceeds from sales to benefit BTA

Press Release

> ? ARE THESE LICENSE PLATES FOR CARS OR BICYCLES? THE AUTHOR DOESN'T SAY.

A new "Share the Road" license plate is now available for purchase in Oregon. The license plate is intended to promote traffic safety, and to help keep cyclists and pedestrians safe.

The plates, which feature the silhouette of a cyclist and a "Share the Road" message, cost $10 (plus a $15 plate replacement fee if you're between renewals). Proceeds from the sale of the plates will be distributed to the BTA and Cycle Oregon. At least 500 plates will need to be sold each year in order to continue to have them available.

> ? WHAT IS BTA? I KNOW ABOUT CYCLE OREGON, BUT I'VE NEVER HEARD OF BTA, AND THE AUTHOR IS NOT TELLING ME.

The plate was created as a result of the passage of Oregon Senate Bill 789-A, sponsored by Sen. Floyd Prozanski, D-Eugene. The idea for the bill came when Prozanski's friend and riding partner Jane Higdon was killed while riding her bike, and he wanted to make an improvement in traffic safety.

BTA Executive Director Scott Bricker comments about the new plates, "sharing the road is a vital message, and we think people who both ride and drive will buy these plates as a way to raise awareness. We encourage everyone to buy one and spread the message that Oregonians share the road."

Jerry Norquist, Executive Director of Cycle Oregon, adds: "Our eventual goal is to be the first state with a public policy that requires 'Share the Road' to be included on every license plate issued."

Order your plate today by visiting ODOT's website.

Source: http://www.earthshare-oregon.org/our-groups/profiles/bta/newsstory.2008-01-11.4822607756

> I REMEMBER READING ABOUT THAT ACCIDENT. I THOUGHT IT WAS CAUSED BY RIDING ON A NARROW ROAD WHEN A BIG TRUCK TRIED TO PASS HER.
>
> ? HOW WOULD A LICENSE PLATE HELP PREVENT THIS?

> OKAY, TO RAISE SAFETY AWARENESS IN DRIVERS TO SHARE THE ROAD WITH BICYCLISTS. I GET IT.
>
> NO FURTHER QUESTIONS.

Many teachers recognize the power of relating out-of-school events to in-school assignments. We also know that most students have some curiosity about their teachers as real people with a life outside of school. Let's capitalize on this curiosity to help us teach questioning skills.

I like to bring to class something that I am reading at home and use it to model how a veteran, adult reader reads it. Using an authentic book or article that I find useful or interesting is a strong tool for modeling reading strategies, such as those for generating questions.

For example, I used an article (see page 43) I had recently read that had grabbed my attention. I inserted questions that arose as I read it. You will notice that I am planting the "author seed" in my first two questions.

By bringing this article to class, making copies for each student, and reading it aloud as they follow along, I model for them how a reader generates questions in a genuine reading, as opposed to only a "school reading." It feels more authentic, less contrived. The three questions I asked are "thick" questions, that is, they seek information beyond what the author provided. Thick questions require readers to be on the ball to notice any gaps in their understanding.

QtM/QtC/QtT/QtA

In this simple activity, a student pauses in his or her reading to write a "Question to Me" (QtM), to a character while reading fiction (QtC), to their teacher (QtT), or to the author (QtA). (See box on page 45 for definitions and examples.) The purpose of this array of questions is for students to recognize trouble spots when reading. The recipient of their questions is less important than the act of question-asking.

Sixth-Grade Whale Riders

Tom Cantwell used this activity when his students were reading the wonderful novel *The Whale Rider* by Witi Ihimaera (1987) in his language arts block. (The book was made into an award-winning movie in 2002.) Tom decided to have students listen to the audio version of the book because it had a narrator who spoke in the same dialect as the characters. His students followed along for the first the few chapters. Hearing the sound of the language made the opening chapters come alive for his kids.

Definitions and Examples

Q TO ME (QtM) questions are those that I ask to myself as I read. Examples: What am I supposed to be getting here? Why am I feeling confused? What should I remember about this part of the reading?

Q TO CHARACTER (QtC) questions are those addressed to a character in the story: Why did you (the character) do such a thing? Didn't you realize that she (another character) already knew the truth? When will you admit that you made a mistake?

Q TO TEACHER (QtT) questions are questions to you, their teacher: Mr./Ms. _____, why is this book telling me something different from what you said in class the other day? Teacher, do I need to know all these details in this section or just the main point?

Q TO AUTHOR (QtA) questions are addressed to the person who wrote this for us: Author, why are you repeating information in paragraph three that you already told me earlier? Author, this part is confusing; can't you be more clear about the causes of oxidation?

At appropriate breaks in the first chapter of the novel, Tom paused the recording and instructed his students to write questions about the "fuzzy parts" on a piece of note-taking paper divided into four sections: two on the front for "Author" and "Characters" and two on the back for "Teacher" and "Me" (see Figure 2.1).

Tom's student Sahalie changed the name of the first category from Questions to Me to Questions to Reader (Me). She tracked her comprehension by noting her confusion over a vocabulary term used in the chapter, her difficulty keeping track of a character, and a few questions about events:

- Why use "fluted"?

- Why did Nanny Flowers hate the telephone?

- Is the spear the same spear that was in the ground?

The class used the category Questions to My Teacher less frequently, but these questions reveal confusion about the new characters that could be cleared up from their teacher:

- Who is the narrator?

- Who is Waori? Who is Rehau?

- Why are we reading this book?

Figure 2.1 Students' author and character questions for *The Whale Rider*

The following questions, addressed to the title character in *The Whale Rider*, show that this student is actively engaged with the story:

- WR: What's the big deal with a human coming?

- WR: Is the spear actually buried?

The goal of this activity, as with all the other activities presented in this book, is what Ciardellio calls "the arousal of curiosity and its positive effect on student performance." If readers are not curious as they read, they are merely looking at the words on a page instead of actually reading them.

Tom's sixth graders enjoyed asking the characters questions most of all. Many of them addressed questions to the main character, Kahu, a young Maori girl:

- How does it feel to be a girl when Koro [her grandfather] wanted a boy to be born?

- How can you still love Koro so much, even though he ignores you and is mean?

- How did you know to bite Koro's toe?

- Why do you cry whenever something bad happens to whales?

- How do you know how to speak to the whales?

- Do you still not like modern foods and things like soda, and if not, why not?

- What was it like living with your other family compared to this one?

- What's the best thing about having Rawiri come back home?

- What do you think the best part about having a sister will be?

They also posed questions to the other important supporting characters in the book: Koro, Jeff, Nanny Flowers, and Rawiri.

One student suggested a new category, Questions to Google, because he realized that the information he needed about the Maori people was surely available on the Internet, and the popular search engine could lead him to it. When students begin to invent their own categories of questions, encourage them by celebrating their progress.

Many students also wrote questions to the author, and they did so quite naturally. I was pleased that they were comfortable addressing the human being who wrote this book, even though they had never previously done so. (See Figure 2.2.)

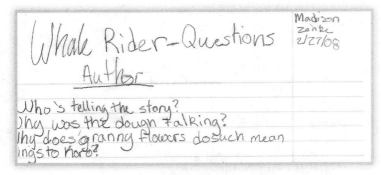

Figure 2.2 Madison's questions to the author about *The Whale Rider*

Using the Character Questions to Role-Play an Interview

After the students have listed their questions, teachers have several options:

- Collect the papers and score them using a point system you like.

- Before collecting them, tell students to mark their two or three favorite questions with an asterisk and get together with a partner to compare and contrast their starred questions in each category, using the conversation to extend understanding.

- Put students into groups of four or five and conduct a mock interview where they take turns at role-playing the character, the teacher, or even the author.

- Send the questions to the author and request some answers. For detailed ideas on how to pull this off, please see my book *Reading Response That Really Matters to Middle Schoolers* (2006).

Tom opted for the mock interview. The students had written questions for five characters, so it made sense to put students in groups of five.

WHAT TO DO WHEN GROUPING GOES BADLY

At first, Tom let students self-select their groups, with the stipulation that "no one will be rejected by any group." Unfortunately, during the two minutes he allotted them to form the groups, he twice observed a student not being welcomed into a group, so he told the class to return to their assigned seats, and he would have to use a different method of grouping. He decided on a random drawing, using tongue depressors with student names printed on them. He drew five at a time, and that was that.

But before they joined their assigned groups, Tom wisely modeled for them how to conduct an interview with a character. He role-played the interviewer, and deputized me to play the interviewee, Kahu, the *Whale Rider* character. Tom posed several questions to me, and I had to "get into character" and think up answers that sounded plausible and interesting. It was harder than I expected! (See box on page 50.)

After our modeling, the students quickly broke into their assigned groups and decided who would play each character. Tom printed out the list of character questions, cut it into strips by character, and randomly handed them to individual group members, making sure they didn't get the questions intended for their character.

Then they started interviewing each other, one character at a time. Tom selected the character Jeff to be the first. Each student in every group got to ask a question of the student assigned the role of Jeff, and "Jeff" answered them. The activity went well, with lots of positive energy and enthusiasm. Students had enough information to answer from the character's perspective, and the teacher modeling helped them get into the role-playing mind set (see Figure 2.3).

During the whole-class debriefing session, everyone agreed that the activity was fun and worth doing again. Tom believes the benefit of this style of reading instruction "is that kids can put themselves into the minds of the characters and author better. In traditional models, students are answering questions and responding from a removed third-person point of view. Here they inject themselves directly into the story by having a direct dialogue with the key players, utilizing the rarely practiced second person ("you"). Perhaps what my students enjoyed the most was getting into first person and actually answering other students' questions as if they were that character or author. Kids, and all people for that matter, enjoy something more when they can take ownership of it, and that's certainly true of this questioning approach to literature."

Figure 2.3 Students answering questions while role-playing characters

The only dissatisfaction students voiced was over the groupings, so Tom had to remind them that they had not followed the directions for choosing groups on their own, so he was forced to switch to random groupings (see box on page 49). He assured them, however, that next time he would consider letting them try again at self-selection.

How to Troubleshoot a Teacher Role-Play With "Negative Modeling"

When I first role-played the character, it would have been good to intentionally give a very short response to one of Tom's questions, so that the kids could hear a *minimal answer*. Then Tom could have asked the class if anyone could offer some elaboration—either from the text, from their imagination, or both—to assist me. Doing this might have encouraged them to provide longer, more complex answers in their own interviews. I call this "negative modeling"—showing students how not to do something, and challenging them to do better.

Next Steps

Tom thinks that next time, after finishing the book, students can view the movie version of the book. Then they can write their questions and interview the author, the film's director, the young actress who plays the protagonist, the whale (!), or a real Maori chief. This would provide a new spin on the activity and inspire even more enthusiasm for question-asking.

Science Students Ask the Tough Questions

Amy Miller, an academic intervention teacher, used a modified QtM/QtT/QtA activity with her seventh and eighth graders to heighten their interest in reading a chapter in their science textbook. Here is how she introduced the activity to the students:

> "You will be reading an assigned chapter for your science class. As you read, you are going to practice asking questions about what you are reading. This skill will help keep your mind actively involved and engaged with the reading."

She gave them three categories instead of four, eliminating questions to characters because they do not apply to science, and instructed them to come up with ten questions in which each of the three types was represented.

Instead of telling her students to use sectioned notebook paper as Tom had in his literature lesson, Amy supplied them with sticky notes for their questions. She intended to color-code the question types, but the school office only had yellow rectangular ones. Instead, she used three different-shaped sticky notes left over from Teacher Appreciation Week (see Figure 2.4).

Figure 2.4 A seventh grader's science Questions to Me

An eighth grader wrote two salient questions on heart-shaped notes: "Why am I confused?" and "Constructive & Destructive forces are different. So why aren't they just called anti- or non-constructive?" (See Figure 2.5.)

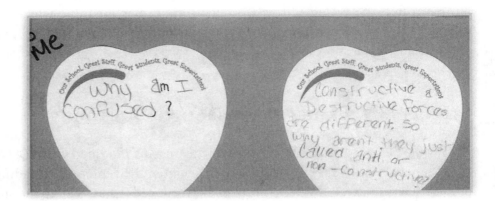

Figure 2.5 An eighth grader's Questions to Me

You will notice that both students used the word *I* in their Questions to Me. Interestingly, though, I could imagine these same two questions being addressed to the author. In fact, many of their questions could go in several categories. This is not a problem, though, because the important factor here is the question-asking, not the particular category. The categories merely serve to stimulate question-asking.

Here are some questions students wrote to their teacher:

- Why does the jellyfish sting you if you touch the tentacles?
- What does it mean when it says 'mate with each other and produce offspring'?
- Will we be learning more about animals?

And the last category, Questions to the Author included:

- Do jellyfish have bones?
- So how are jellyfish born?
- Why do you put a lot of non-necessary info in here?
- Why are there random pictures of rocks here?

One student asked:

> ◉ Why would people die within four minutes of getting stung by a jelly fish when in *SpongeBob* [*SquarePants*] it just gives them a little shock?

And a bit of advice to the author, instead of a question:

> ◉ I think you could have talked more and explained more about adaptations for getting food.

Amy's students liked the novelty of question-asking better than routine question-answering. They liked having choices with the question categories, and they surely appreciated the sticky notes. Additionally, and this is important, she picked reading selections that the kids found highly interesting. What's not to like about the mating patterns of jellyfish?

SOME TEACHING TIPS FOR THIS ACTIVITY

1. Instead of merely assigning the types of questions, begin by modeling them to your students. You begin reading the assignment and stop periodically to ask a question. I recommend actually writing your questions, so that they can see you doing it. You could write them on the board, on the overhead, or onto your computer connected to a projection device.

2. To motivate your students to generate questions, provide them with colored sticky notes—a different color (or shape) for each of the categories. In fact, when you model the procedure to them (Step 1, above) you could draw large stickies onto an overhead transparency, so that they can see what you are doing and remember that each color or shape is for a different type of question.

3. Also, to motivate them, try this technique out: Tell them that questioning while reading is a key comprehension aid. Point out that good readers are constantly asking questions in order to stay focused and alert.

4. **A further incentive:** Offer them points for each question. You might tell them that each question they write is worth one point, or perhaps award one point for QtM, two points for QtC/T, and three points for QtA. Alternatively, tell them they must ask questions totaling 10 points, and it's up to them to decide which category or categories to write.

5. Tell your students to make sure to address the proper person when writing a question in a category. Remind them to use key words like *I, you, Teacher, Ms. _____.* (See box on page 47.)

6. Instead of showing them all four types at once, you could teach one category at a time.

7. Feel free to modify anything here and do your own thing.

Thin and Thick Questions

This is my all-time favorite student-questioning activity. I have been using it and advocating its use for 15 years or so. It is a valuable activity for supporting comprehension that students quickly grasp.

For years I believed I had invented this activity until I discovered a few years ago that I actually renamed terms from Spencer Kagan's "Fat and Skinny" questions (1994). Those terms made me feel a bit uncomfortable, so I replaced them with the softer Thin and Thick. So, thanks Dr. Kagan for the great idea.

Okay, the definitions:

Definitions and Examples

Thin questions are literal questions whose answers are readily available in the text. You ask yourself these questions to check your understanding: "Do I understand what the author is telling me?"

Thick questions are more open-ended or interpretive, between the lines, or "below-the-surface," as Ciardiello calls them. You ask them to push yourself beyond the text and toward a more advanced understanding, by adding some information, by hypothesizing, speculating, or inferring: "Do I understand what the author is NOT telling me?"

As you can see, this activity brings the author into the questioning because both types of questions consider the author as the source, or partial source, of information. As we've seen before, bringing the author into students' consciousness forces them to think about the assigned reading in terms of what information they are and are not getting from the author.

Perhaps the simplest way to familiarize students with Thin and Thick questions is to liken them to easy and hard questions. Here are questions a fifth grader in Greg Taylor's class at McGovern Elementary School in Winston, Oregon, wrote after reading an article in literature textbook called The Dolphin and the Diver. Note the circled *E* and *H* labels for "easy" and "hard." (See Figure 2.6)

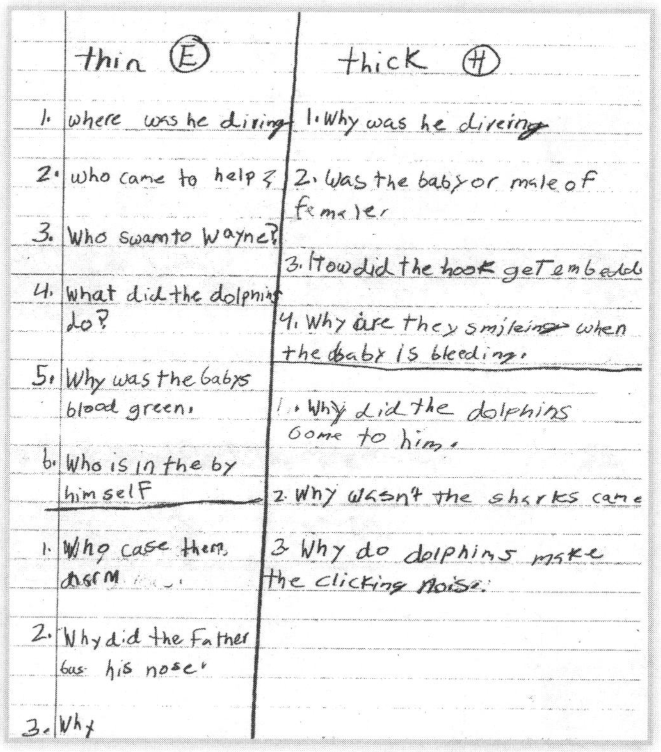

Figure 2.6 Thin and Thick questions for "The Dolphin and the Diver"

Questioning Nessie in an Intervention Class

Amy Miller assigned her seventh and eighth graders an article about the Loch Ness Monster. She told them that good readers constantly ask themselves questions as they are reading. In fact, active, alert readers *cannot stop* asking questions when reading. Next, she told them there are two types of questions good readers can ask: Thin and Thick. She asked if anyone knew the difference between the two. After a few good guesses, she provided the definitions.

After reading the first paragraph to her class, she paused to model how to ask a Thin question. Next, Amy asked the class to answer the question and to explain why the question is considered Thin. The students responded that the author provided the answer clearly. Amy created a large, two-columned chart to show the difference between Thin and Thick questions and to record questions for each type. Then she guided the questioning. Here are some student-generated Thin questions:

- What did Harold Doc Edgerton scan the water with?

- How long has Nessie been around for?

- Who captured the "monster"?

Why would a teacher want her students to generate Thin questions that are easily answered from information right in the text? Two reasons:

> 1. **To build confidence.** Students can say, "I read this assignment, and I understood it enough to ask questions that I can answer."
>
> 2. **To recall information.** Thin questions serve as solid review questions.

Amy was surprised to discover that generating Thin questions was not that easy for her students. As she explained, "I had to point them in the direction of focusing their questions on the theme or main idea of the article because some students were taking random pieces of information that weren't very important and using those as Thin questions. They were Thin, but they weren't very focused. And some students would merely copy information literally and not even reword it into a question that made sense. I found it interesting that coming up with Thin questions was a little more difficult than Thick!"

Hmmm. This is surprising to me, too, because literal-level questions should be easier to generate than those on the inferential level. To help her students, Amy borrowed an idea from Julie LaConte, a teacher at Hoech Middle School in St. Louis, and made a chart showing the different question starters for each type (see box on page 57).

Thin and Thick Question Starters

Thin questions usually begin with *Who, What, When, Where,* and *How does?*

Thick questions often begin with *How, Why, Who might, What will, What if,* and *I wonder why.*

Source: Julie LaConte, Hoech Middle School, St. Louis

Amy repeated the procedure for Thick questions, first defining them, next modeling, then discussing, and finally turning them over to her students to try. Here are some student-generated Thick questions:

- How can the sonar detect so many meters from the boat?

- What will they think of next?

- Would they harm Nessie if they found him?

- Why didn't they take the photo to prove it?

The kids clearly benefited from the list of starter words, but you'll notice that the second question begins with "What," which is actually a Thin starter word. In this way, the list serves as a starting point and not a rigid formula. Thin words can begin with Thick starters, and vice versa.

And why have students generate Thick questions that cannot be answered with information from the text? Two reasons:

1. To push readers to think beyond the text

2. To make students aware that the textbook, or any single resource, may not provide all necessary information on a topic

Introducing Thin and Thick Questions

Evan Chandler came up with a great way to introduce these two types of questions to his sixth graders. He wrote a paragraph about his life as a student and as a teacher along with six questions and Thin and Thick categories. His instructions read: "Put an X on the Thin or Thick side to show where each question belongs." (See Figure 2.7.) Evan knew that answering teacher-generated questions was an essential first step in familiarizing his class with Thin and Thick questions.

Next, he assigned a short reading from the novel *Dar and the Spear Thrower* followed by student-generated Thin and Thick questions (see Figure 2.8). Assigning a short passage is an effective way of easing students into independent question-asking.

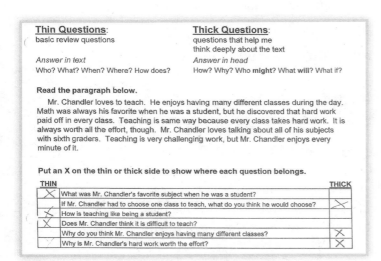

Figure 2.7 Evan's paragraph with questions for students to sort

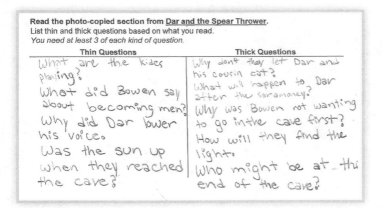

Figure 2.8 Thin and Thick questions about *Dar and the Spear Thrower*

Thin and Thick With Literature

Cody Loy, a language arts teacher at Cal Young Middle School, Eugene, Oregon, used Thin questions for reviewing previous readings in John Steinbeck's *The Pearl*, but he also employed "serious and complex Thicks when generating class discussion and personal responses following the readings. This story develops slowly and can be very subtle at times when alluding, and referring, to some of the bigger issues, like themes, that the author wants the reader to see." I like how Cody brought the author into the lesson.

Let's Get Physical: A Helpful Modification for Students Learning Thin and Thick

Evan found that his sixth graders had some difficulty applying Thin and Thick questions to literature. "The students were moderately engaged in this activity, but they struggled with generating their own questions, which seemed to detract from their enthusiasm for the activity."

So Evan made a wise adjustment to help this activity fly. He created a physical response to help students internalize the meaning of Thin and Thick questions. Every time the students heard the phrase "Thin question," they tapped an imaginary text on their desktop three times to indicate that the text provides the answer to that type of query. Upon hearing "Thick question," the students tapped their heads three times to remind themselves that this type of inquiry would be answered through their own critical thinking. He reports, "This physical response seemed to be very effective for helping the students remember the two categories of questions." Nice improvement.

Evan also recognized that he needed to ease his students into question-asking by providing a three-step scaffolded procedure. After discussing the definitions and examples of Thin and Thick questions, Evan used the class's shared read-aloud novel to generate some real-life examples of each kind of question. The following day, the students read a paragraph about the teacher and sorted pre-written questions into the Thin or Thick category. Finally, he photocopied a page from the read-aloud book and had students read it and generate three questions in each category.

Most of Evan's students had no trouble sorting the questions, but many still struggled with generating their own. It's important to remember that some middle graders will struggle more than we might expect and will require more instruction and practice. To me, the source of this difficulty is the traditional role of questioning in the classroom, in which questions derive from the teacher or the book, and students encounter them *after* reading, as a comprehension check. Thin and Thick questioning turns the tables by giving the question-asking power to the kids as they read. Great, but this may not be an easy transaction for them. That's why we keep trying, why we use lots of different activities, and why we sometimes must adapt, modify, and adjust them.

Thin and Thick Questions in a Science Class

Here is another solid modification from Annie Cooper, a science teacher who uses Thin and Thick questions to support reading comprehension. Her students wanted her to be more specific about what Thin and Thick meant, so she gave them examples from a book they were reading in language arts before they started on the science reading assignment. Good idea, because while it is easy to ask Thin questions about a subject like science, Thick ones are much harder to think up.

Annie led the students through the first three paragraphs, and after each one, they jointly came up with a Thin and Thick question, using Julie LaConte's sentence starters (see page 57). After they had copied down the first three from the board, Annie had them do it on their own. Of course, her students wanted to work together, but she thought it was important for them to work individually to stretch them and force them to think a little more.

Her kids realized that they could find the answers to most of the Thin questions in the book, but that answering the Thick questions might require more research. Her colleague Emily Robbins discovered that the directive to "read between the lines" for Thick questions was too challenging for her ESL students, who don't yet understand many American idioms. They also struggled to understand the meaning of *interpretive*, but found Julie LaConte's question starters helpful. She also discovered that the Thick questions many kids wrote were really questions for further study. The questions didn't require interpretation, just additional information that could be found elsewhere, such as:

- How many dams are on the Columbia?

- Who built the dams?

I see the difference she is pointing out, but I don't have a problem with these questions being labeled Thick. But Emily suggests creating a third category: "Questions for further research." Some high school teachers have added a more advanced category called Thickest questions. Both are interesting modifications. Emily's suggestion also reminds me of Questions to Google in the previous section. The best way to go, of course, is whichever way feels the most useful to your students. None of the procedures in these questioning activities are written in stone; it's up to you to decide how best to implement them.

What to Do With Thin and Thick Questions

Emily's idea of an extended category leads me to a final consideration of this activity. After students generate their questions, what might a teacher do with them?

First off, most students I've worked with want to know right away if they have to answer their questions after writing them. I like to shock kids, so I always say, "No, all you have to do is write them." This typically prompts another question from them: "You mean all we have to do is make up questions? We don't have to answer them??" "That's right," I reply. "Wait a minute," they say. "The assignment is just to write questions but not answer them?" When I reply in the affirmative, I usually get a quiet smirking reaction because they think asking questions is easier than answering them.

I disagree, but, hey, if they are motivated by the perception that this is an easy assignment, I'm cool with that. Once students read and generate the questions, we have lots of choices of what to do next.

1. You can score them, awarding one point for Thins and two points for Thicks.

2. Put kids into pairs and have them swap questions. If students have trouble answering each other's Thin questions, allow them to review the reading assignment. Since Thick questions are not explicitly answered in the text, they must discuss these answers with their partner. That's *discuss,* not argue.

3. When students come up with good questions, I sometimes use them on a test or quiz. When I do this, I reward the student with a bonus point for a Thin question and two points for a Thick one.

4. Instead of having students record their questions on a worksheet, provide them with two colors of paper strips, or even better, two colors of 3" x 5" cardstock rectangles, with instructions to write *Thins* on one color and *Thicks* on the other. Again, you can require a certain number of each type. Then place the kids into groups of four to six to play a card game.

5. For those *Super-Thick* questions that no one in the room (including you) can answer, deputize a student or students to answer it through alternative sources for extra-credit homework. Be sure to set a time frame, require that the source(s) be cited, and review Internet research skills. I require students to use educational subject directories, like Yahooligans and Brainboost, instead of general search engines, like Google.

6. I love assigning students to write to their author with questions. My earlier book, *Reading Response That Really Matter to Middle Schoolers* (2006), provides multiple ways of having kids "talk back" to authors.

Thin, Thick, and Sidekick

Terry Kennedy, a sixth-grade teacher at Twin Peaks School in Tucson, Arizona, assigned her class to read a short story I wrote about a cat named Sidd who must go to the vet for an eye problem (see box on page 63). To enable her students to attain maximum comprehension through independent reading, she embedded questions into the text. Because she downloaded this story from my Web site, she was able to insert questions into the story and to highlight tricky vocabulary in red.

Adding a Level

Terry began with Thin and Thick questions because her students were familiar with them. Building on what they already know provides solid scaffolding for taking your students to the next level of questioning.

The answer to the second Thin question "Who is Sidd?" (See box on page 63) is clear from reading the story, while the Thick one about the character Inga is harder because the story does not provide that information yet.

The embedded questions served to prompt the students to generate their own questions while reading and to label them "Thin" or "Thick." One student asked, "Why does the vet shine the light in Sidd's face?" indicates that she doesn't know this procedure for checking eyes. Since the author did not see fit to provide an explanation, the question is a Thick one for this student.

Another student wrote a Thicker question: "Why does Sidd usually watch TV?" This is a very good question because the author does not explain why Sidd partakes in this odd habit for a cat.

Later in the story, Terry bumped up her expectations for their reading by inserting what I call a Sidekick question for her students: "Why did you [the author] write about a cat that supposedly can read?"

Sidekick questions are addressed directly to the author, for the following reasons:

1. **to inquire about missing information or to seek additional background information**

2. **for a justification/rationale for a decision the author made in writing the story**

This type of question asks readers to find out from the author what he or she was thinking when writing a particular piece. Sidekick questions provide students with a golden opportunity to ask themselves, "Do I need more information from the author to help me understand where he or she is coming from with this writing?" Sidekicks are at a deeper level of questioning than Thins and Thicks because they seek to clarify why an author did or did not provide certain information.

Excerpt from:

Sidd's Excellent Adventure

By Leon LeWine

For me, taking a cat to the vet is routine. I've done it many, many times in my life already. See, we've owned many cats. And every time it's the same: look all over the place for the cat; find the cat hiding because it somehow knows it's vet time; coax the cat out using food; grab suspicious little kitty; carry it to the car; toss it in the back seat; try to drive safely even though the cat now has crawled to the front and is trying to hide beneath the brake pedal; reach the vet's office; carry the cat into the waiting room; listen to the shrieks of resentment; and finally, take pussy cat into the exam room to greet the vet. A hundred times, I'll bet. And every time it was the same. Until last time.

THIN: WHO IS SIDD?

Our latest cat, Sidd, needed his annual checkup, and since he's a bit large for one adult human to handle, both Inga and I went through the routine: look all over for Sidd; find Sidd hiding under the rose bush; coax Sidd out using Mouse-o-Snaks; grab suspicious Sidd; etc. etc.

THIN: WHY DOES THE NARRATOR KNOW SO MUCH ABOUT GOING TO THE VET?

THICK: WHO IS INGA?

Everything went according to routine until the end of the exam when Inga told the vet that Sidd was having some trouble with his eyes. He was blinking a lot, and when he sat in our laps, he no longer watched us read like he usually did; he just stared off into space. And television wasn't any big deal for him anymore.

So the vet looks, and pokes, and looks again. "Could be a clogged tear duct. I'll check it." He leaves the exam room to get something. Sidd yowls, Inga pets him, and I wonder how many more trips to the vet are ahead for me.

("Sidd's Excellent Adventure" and a second version of it, "Sidd, the Super Cat" are both are available to teachers on my Web site: http://www.larrylewin.com/teachingresources/shortstories.html)

Thin, Thick, and Sidekick questions represent a hierarchy of thinking because each successive type builds upon the others:

- Thin questions ask about information provided by the author.

- Thick questions ask about information not completely provided by the author.

- Sidekick questions ask the author directly about the reasons information was or was not provided.

Why do I call them Sidekick questions? A sidekick is a loyal companion, a friend, an attentive assistant, a buddy who is there to help. I think of Dr. Watson being there for Sherlock Holmes, Barney Rubble for Fred Flintstone, and Thelma for Louise. I like the idea of students playing the role of sidekick to an author, there to help him or her notice any problems with the text, areas of potential confusion for the reader, or even some polite suggestions. Obviously, the sidekick relationship is different from what students are accustomed to: reading the assignment and answering the questions afterward. I prefer Sidekick questions because the student-reader moves next to the author, not in opposition to the author.

My lovely Sidekick label may not resonate with students because they may not be familiar with the term, so I ask them if they know the word "Sidekick". If not, I search Google Images for photos of icons of Sidekickery to show the kids. That quickly brings them up to speed.

Terry's sixth graders took right to sidekicking; notice how many included the word *you* in the questions they wrote about "Sidd's Excellent Adventure."

- Would you consider explaining more what the narrator is thinking?

- I am wondering if the narrator gets in trouble a lot and how often?

- Would you consider adding another setting instead of only at the vet's office?

- Did you consider adding another character? Two fat house cats doing this would be funnier.

- I am wondering if you really think Sidd the Cat can read?

- Why didn't you tell us what was wrong with Sidd's face?

- Did you mean to make it seem that Inga understands what the vet is saying?

Perhaps you noticed a few of them plugged in the starter phrase "I am wondering" from the earlier wonderment questions in the preceding chapter (see Chapter 1). I am very pleased when the various questioning activities overlap because flexibility increases students' questioning ability. It is clear that these readers are really on their toes when they're reading. These kids are actively involved in taking the author's words from the text and constructing meaning in their minds. Terry reported that she had trouble stopping her kids from asking questions! Nod your head if you like the idea of your students thinking as they read. Kind of important to comprehension, yes?

Sidekick Question Starters

You will notice that Terry's students benefited from the following list of Sidekick question starters. All the prompts include the word *you* in them. Providing some scaffolding will help when teaching students a new technique like this.

- Why did you (author) . . .

- Why didn't you . . .

- Will you please tell me . . .

- Did you ever consider . . .

- Would you consider . . .

- I am wondering if you . . .

- Do you think it might be better if . . .

- Are you implying . . .

This last one, invented by Jared, a student in Terry's class, was a great way to begin a Sidekick question: "Are you implying that the narrator might be color blind?"

The following questions demonstrate how some readers need a better understanding of the main character, the narrator:

- Do you think it would be better if the [main] character was more immature?

- Do you think it would be better if you told more about the narrator?

I have heard this request from middle-grade readers so often that I was inspired to write a different version of the story with more description of this character.

Fourth Graders Try Sidekick Questions

John Waldron, a teacher at Paul W. Kutz Elementary School in Doylestown, Pennsylvania, had to made some adaptations to Sidekick questions for his fourth graders. Because the Sidd stories were a bit above their reading level, and due to time constraints, John read the stories aloud to the whole class. As he read, he periodically stopped to ask Thin, Thick, and Sidekick questions. Since his students already knew about the first two types, they were able to generate their own Thin questions:

- What made the cat's eye glow?

- How does Sidd feel about the vet?

- What was the setting of the story?

- What is a tear duct? (Actually this could be considered a Thick question because the author did not provide the answer in the story.)

Here are some Thick questions they wrote while reading the story:

- Why do you think animals know when they are going to the vet?

- What if Sidd became an evil superhero?

- How might you act if you were Sidd?

- Do you think the eye drops hurt Sidd? Why or why not?

- What do you think would happen if they were allowed to continue playing in the exam room?

- Which story do you like better? Why?

When they tried asking Sidekick questions, some of them were overly general, like the first three that follow:

- What inspired you to write this story?

- Was this story based on a real-life event?

- What is the purpose of this story?

- Did you consider using another pet, like a dog, instead of a cat? Why?

- Why did you rewrite the story?

- Why did you mix reality with fantasy?

- How did you get the idea of a cat reading?

- Why did you switch the characters to a mother and son?

These questions did not surprise me. While these fourth graders' questions were more general, they were appropriate to these students' stage of development.

Thinking ahead to future assignments, John commented, "I would probably select different stories at a more independent reading level if I did this activity for another group." Indeed, it's a good idea to carefully match text readability to student readiness. John came up with three good instructional ideas worth considering when you try this activity:

1. He started the activity by reviewing the term *sidekick* with examples like Batman and Robin, Yogi Bear and Boo Boo, and the Lightning McQueen and Mater the Tow Truck from the movie *Cars,* which his students found enjoyable and engaging. (Images of these characters are available on the Internet.)

2. To ease them into the activity, he read the stories aloud to the whole group, with individual students generating their own questions.

3. He formed small groups that came together to select their best questions, which were then recorded on a single sheet by the group "secretary." Each group then shared its best question in each category with the class. The Sidekick questions took the most time since they were new to the kids.

Riding Sidekick Through Nonfiction Reading

Of course, readers also can ask Sidekick questions of an author of nonfiction/informational text. Here is an excerpt from the end of a disturbing *National Geographic* article from their Web site about the mining of the mineral coltan in Africa for use in cell phones. I copied the article from the site, pasted it into my word processing program, and inserted a Thick question and two Sidekicks.

You can do the same for an article in your social studies, math, or science class. Alternatively, you could photocopy the text and hand-write questions into the margins. Or, you could use sticky notes for the questions.

Excerpt from:

E-Waste

by Stefan Lovgren

**THICK ?
WHAT IS WRONG WITH THROWING AWAY AN OLD CELL PHONE?**

Sharon Dewar, a spokesperson for the San Diego Zoo, says the objective of the recycling program is conservation education.

"Many people have cell phones at home in a drawer that are old, and they don't know what to do with them," she said.

"These phones contain toxic elements. What we're saying is, Please don't throw your cell phone into a landfill."

"If a cell phone can be refurbished, that might also help diminish the demand for coltan mining, which could in fact help gorillas and other animals in their habitat," she said.

To Ronay, the Eco-Cell president, used cell phones are only one part of a growing e-waste problem.

"No one really understands how critical this is going to be, especially as technology progresses and more technology becomes abandoned," he said.

"We are going to look up one day and be in the middle of a crisis."

**SIDEKICK ?
STEFAN, DID YOU DECIDE TO RESEARCH THIS ISSUE AND WRITE THIS ARTICLE, OR DID *NATIONAL GEOGRAPHIC* MAGAZINE THINK OF THE IDEA AND ASSIGN YOU TO RESEARCH AND WRITE IT?**

Mendelev's Periodic Table and the Eighth-Grade Science Students Who Study It

When Annie Cooper assigned her eighth-grade science students an article on the periodic table of the elements, she employed the three-column method of recording questions (see Figure 2.9).

Since the article was pretty advanced for eighth grade—I used the Lexile Analyzer at lexile.com and found that the Lexile Level was 1160, a low tenth-grade level—Annie decided to read it together as a class. "The kids actually found it interesting," Annie reported. "Especially the part where Mendelev was a cheese-factory inspector in Russia." An interesting topic goes a long way in motivating students to read carefully.

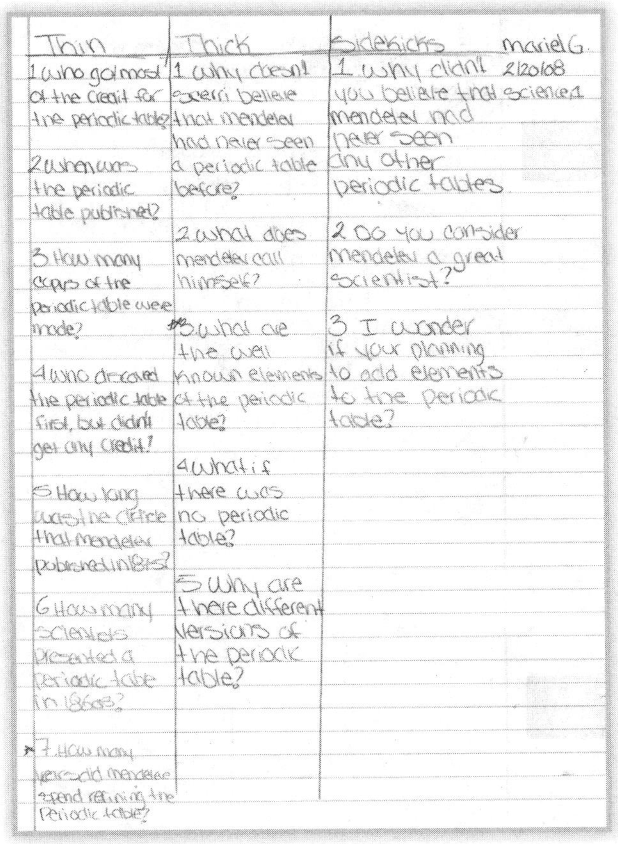

Thin	Thick	Sidekicks mariel G. 2/20/08
1 who got most of the credit for the periodic table?	1 why doesn't Scerri believe that mendelev had never seen a periodic table before?	1 why didn't you believe that scienced mendelev had never seen any other periodic tables
2 when was the periodic table published?	2 what does mendelev call himself?	2 do you consider mendelev a great scientist?
3 How many copys of the periodic table were made?	*3 what are the well known elements of the periodic table?	3 I wonder if your planning to add elements to the periodic table?
4 who discoved the periodic table first, but didn't get any credit?	4 what if there was no periodic table?	
5 How long was the article that mendelev published in 1871?	5 Why are there different versions of the periodic table?	
6 How many scientists presented a periodic table in 1860s?		
*7 How many years did mendelev spend refining the periodic table?		

Figure 2.9 Three-column questions on the periodic table

It is clear that asking questions helped children understand the rather sophisticated ideas in this article. Before Annie had them share in groups, she had students decide on their best questions for the author and mark them with stars. Here are some of them:

- Why did you disagree with the idea that Mendelev created the periodic table?
- Why did you want to continue the elements?
- Why didn't you make the periodic table smaller?
- Will you please tell me why you don't believe Mendelev and his work?
- Would you consider writing more information on each element?
- Why did you mention that Mendelev developed the oil industry?

Summary

I have presented the four types of question-asking activities discussed in this chapter in order of complexity. All four of these activities bring the author into the questioning. This is because directing questions to the author, or considering what the author did or didn't do, motivates students to ask questions. It makes questioning more relevant, more important. Now we turn to two classic questioning frameworks that have been inspiring both teachers and students for years.

CHAPTER 3

Classic Questioning Frameworks

> ● I think my "Author and Me" questions were the best because there were lots of clues to help answer the questions.
>
> ~ Molly, Eighth-Grade Social Studies Student

No book on student questioning would be complete without a discussion of Question-Answer Relationships (QAR) and Questioning the Author (QtA), two now-classic questioning frameworks renowned for teaching students how to generate questions while reading. This chapter offers a brief overview of each, helpful student question samples, references to more complete resources, and modifications that I have used with middle-grade readers.

Question-Answer Relationships (QAR)

Taffy Raphael began developing this reading comprehension strategy back in 1979. Question-Answer Relationships guide students to examine and discover the sources of answers to various types of questions.

Raphael devised two general categories of question-answers: In the Book and In My Head. The first type of question can be answered with information provided by the author in the reading assignment. In My Head questions require the reader to rely on his or her own knowledge to supplement what the author did not provide in the text. These questions could be labeled "literal" and "inferential," but Raphael's terms are far more descriptive for middle graders because they point readers toward where they must go to answer the question, and they provide a shared vocabulary for discussion.

Raphael and her colleagues subdivide these two QAR categories into four subcategories. They break down In the Book question types this way:

- Right There: "The answer is in one place in the text."

- Think and Search: "The answer is in the text, [but] readers need to...put together different parts of the text to find the answer."

They divide In My Head question types into the following:

- Author and Me: "The answer is not in the text, [so] readers need to think about how the text and what they already know fit together."

- On My Own: "The answer is not in the text. Readers need to use their own ideas and experiences to answer."

Steve Quiring, a science teacher at Lincoln High School in Lincoln, Nebraska, provides his students with an excellent summary of the four types of QAR questions:

QAR Definitions and Examples

In the Book	In My Head
RIGHT THERE Right There questions and their **answers come straight from the text.** These questions often begin with "Who is...?" "What is...?" "When is...?" "What kind of...?" "Name..." or "List..." To answer these questions, readers must locate and copy the information.	**AUTHOR AND ME** Author and Me questions require an **answer that draws on information beyond what the text offers.** Readers must internalize the main ideas of the text before they can elaborate on it. An example of this kind of question in chemistry is "How can you tell if a substance is a metal or nonmetal?" The question assumes the reader is familiar with the properties of metal and nonmetals and can describe a lab test for determining these properties.
THINK AND SEARCH Think & Search questions **require you to read several sentences or sections of text and combine the information to answer the question.** These questions often begin with "Summarize..." "What caused...?" "Contrast..." "Compare..." and "Explain...." You need to put information from several parts of the text together in a meaningful way to answer the question.	**ON MY OWN** On My Own questions require answers that are **not in the book.** For example, "How can plastics be most effectively designed to serve society rather than harm it?" The question requires readers to draw upon their own background knowledge to put together an answer.

Source: http://lhs.lps.org/staff/squiring/chemistry/Intro/QAR.htm

Over the years, QAR has enjoyed widespread popularity with teachers of reading. QAR gives students and teachers a vocabulary for dissecting text information, and I like it because it brings students from the outside of comprehension questions to the inside.

In order for students to truly understand the purpose of QAR, Raphael emphasizes that questions need to serve a purpose. "The kids respond better if they see QAR as a tool for participating in book club discussions, guiding their choice of inquiry questions, making sense of test questions, etc." Kids need to understand the purpose of the questioning so it doesn't feel simply like "more work." I have used QAR with students in language arts classes and various content-area classes to improve self-monitoring of comprehension. In my experience, kids are quick to pick up on this system.

Eighth-Grade Social Studies Lesson

Dorothy Syfert and I taught eighth-grade language arts/social studies blocks next door to one another for years at James Monroe Middle School, in Eugene, Oregon. Periodically, we still get together to discuss school, the challenges of teaching, and the big issues facing education. And whenever one of us learns a new technique, we share it.

I told her I was kicking around a modification of QAR, based on *QAR NOW, A Powerful and Practical Framework That Develops Comprehension and Higher-Level Thinking in All Students* by Raphael, Highfield, and Au (2006). This book served as both a valuable review of the basics of QAR and a source of new information on the subject.

Dorothy, an avid collector of teaching tools, was intrigued with the possibility of using QAR to bolster student engagement and motivation in her U.S. History class. Too often, her students lacked energy and attentiveness when faced with nonfiction reading assignments. Question-answer relationships looked promising for turning this around.

We decided to ask students to read an article titled "No Royal Masters, No Slave Masters." This piece of historical fiction about the Revolutionary War is written in the voice of an escaped slave who argues that freedom and liberty mean nothing unless both black and white colonists can enjoy them.

The QAR Game Plan

I introduced the class to the QAR method by explicitly explaining the purpose and procedure of Question-Answer Relationships.

QAR Six-Step Instructional Model

The creators of QAR suggest that we scaffold instruction by using a six-step instructional model that begins with lots of teacher guidance and gradually places the questioning work in the hands of the students.

1. EXPLICIT EXPLANATION Tell your students you are trying something new that will help them read for better understanding.

TEACHING TIPS

- Tell them it's called QAR, for Question-Answer Relationships. (Write it on the board as well.)
- Tell them there are two categories of questions: In the Book and In My Head.
- In the Book means the answer to the question is found right in the text (book, article, poem, etc.). Draw a picture or symbol such as a book on the board.
- In My Head means the answer to the question must come from the reader's mind or from both the text and the reader's mind. Draw a picture such as a thought bubble to visually indicate this.

2. MODELING Show your students, rather than tell them, how to identify and answer various types of questions.

TEACHING TIPS

- Refer to the assigned passage and demonstrate to your students how you think about the differences between a Right There question and a Think and Search question.
- Likewise, in the same passage, point out your thinking on determining the difference between Author and Me and On My Own questions.

3. GUIDED PRACTICE In guided practice, the class reviews the different types of questions.

TEACHING TIPS

- Present two questions to see if they can identify the difference in question type, especially when teaching the inferential Author and Me and On My Own questions.

4. COACHING Place students in pairs and tell them to work together to read a new passage and develop questions for it.

TEACHING TIPS

⦿ Match students who have approximately the same readiness level to prevent one reader from dominating. Or you may prefer to have students work in groups of three or four.

5. INDEPENDENT APPLICATION Have students read a passage on their own, to generate one type of question, and answer it.

At this point, consider:

⦿ Will students be assigned question types to practice or will they be allowed to choose?

⦿ Will they need extrinsic motivation to tackle the more difficult question types, and if so, would offering extra points provide a built-in incentive?

6. ASSESSMENT AND GOAL SETTING Come together as a whole class and discuss.

⦿ Determine how well they did on Step 5.

⦿ Decide what should be done next.

For more detail on this six-step procedure, see Chapter 2 of *QAR Now*.

 To illustrate the first QAR subcategories, I drew an image of a book on the board as I explained the similarities and differences between Right There and Think and Search.

At this early stage, Dorothy reminded her students that their goal as readers was to "become an adult reader in your head." Self-questioning is a good way to become an "adult reader."

For the second step of the QAR method, modeling, we employed the Reciprocal Teaching technique invented by Annemarie Palinscar and Ann Brown (1984) by reading the title, author, and introductory paragraph aloud to the class and modeling how to ask In the Book questions. I figured it made sense to begin with a Right There question, so after the reading, I asked, "Who is the author of this article?" The students had no trouble supplying the answer because the author's name, Thomas Broder, is listed *right there* at the top. I recorded both the question and their answer on the board, and the students copied them onto notebook paper, identifying the question-type with the label, *RT*.

I next asked a Think and Search question based on the second paragraph: "What does the article's title mean?" I modeled the idea that in order to answer this question, the reader must look in several places to pull together information. The answer lies in the second paragraph as well as in the title. Again, I recorded the question and answer on the board for each student to copy. I then asked for a volunteer to try to generate a different Think and Search question.

At this point, Dorothy interjected another question: "On a test, which type of question is easier to answer: a *Right There* question or a *Think and Search*." The students immediately knew Right There questions are easier to answer, and they could explain why.

Carefully Passing the Ball to the Students

To ease the class into this new approach to reading, after modeling for students, we proceeded into the article using Reciprocal Teaching. I asked for a student volunteer to read the next paragraph and then asked if anyone could make up a Right There type of question, then took my own turn reading a different paragraph and generating one of the question types. This process of alternating back and forth between teacher and student familiarizes students with the QAR method. No need to rush this; building competence and confidence in question-asking is not something that can be accomplished overnight.

After we reached the middle of the article in this manner, I felt ready to up the ante with an Author and Me question: "Why does the author, Thomas Broder, include an advertisement for a slave auction in his article?" I wrote it on the board beneath a simple sketch of a human head to visually represent this second category of questions, In My Head.

As we discussed this question, the students realized that unlike the previous In the Book questions, this one had to be answered with only *a hint* from the author. The term *hint* actually came from a student of Dorothy's named Molly, who said that even though an author does not provide the answer to an Author and Me question, he gives you a hint that can help you figure it out.

One student, Justyn, even created a new hybrid category: A&A, or Author and another Author. The category came about when Justyn was unable to answer an On My Own question and needed an outside source to find the answer. Dorothy and I were thrilled not only because Justyn was showing interest in the topic, but also because this is just what Taffy Raphael writes about in her book: "The important point is that QAR gave [the student] the language with which to pinpoint the specific kind of help he needed, rather than resorting to the vague 'I don't get it' that we often hear in classrooms."

Keep It Simple…Or Else

After this initial training, we began to make the vital shift toward students' generating questions of their own. We based the lesson on an article called "A Loyalist View," from the same resource. To guide the students toward independent questioning, we provided them with a four-category worksheet for recording their questions, known as a QAR Guide (see box). And because the students were already familiar with the "shared language of QAR," the shift from teacher-generated to student-generated questions was smooth. I created the grid by modifying an online resource from social studies teacher Raymond Jones at his Web site, ReadingQuest: Making Sense in Social Studies (http://www.readingquest.org/pdf/qar.pdf).

With apologies to Raphael and her colleagues, I modified some of the question category terms in hopes of creating the perfect label for each type of question-answer relationship. You will see a code for each question types so students could label them more easily.

Question-Answer Relationships Guide	
IN THE TEXT	**IN MY BRAIN**
RH = Right Here (in the paragraph)	**A & M** = Author and Me **I & M** = Illustrator and Me
H & T = Here and There (answer is in a few paragraphs)	**OMO** = On My Own (nothing from the author to help me)

I arranged the codes on a worksheet divided into grids. As much I like my revised QAR codes, not all student agreed with me that the originals needed any improvement. My feelings weren't hurt; I'm much more concerned with the actual question-asking than the codes themselves.

Dorothy and I told the class that the goal here is for them to become alert readers who read for meaning and actively look for obstacles to understanding. Whatever codes you and your students use, keep them consistent to ensure the activity is clear and simple.

We were pleased to find that all the students were able to label their questions. Some did so immediately, others needed some additional assistance from the teacher, but a few resisted. One student complained that doing the question-writing was "very straining and draining of my energy because it hurts my hand" and called the activity "kinda dumb and pointless."

Three thoughts on this. First, some students do not take well to a new activity, especially one that demands thought. This is disappointing, but it happens. Second, the student may have been overwhelmed by the amount of thinking the activity required. This task was to read carefully, think of questions, determine the proper category, record questions in the proper box on the grid, and finally, answer them. Perhaps this was too much to ask from some students. And his "dumb and pointless" comment might mean that the purpose for doing this activity was not clear enough.

Third, and this is critically important, QAR needs to be taught as a simple approach to reading. If it comes across as complicated, it can lose its positive impact. The four types of questions must be clearly defined and modeled. And for some students, it may be wise to keep it at In the Book questions for several sessions without rushing forward. Once they show comfort at this level, assign In My Head questions.

Likewise, some students will benefit from working with a partner to generate questions before meeting in a group (see box on page 81). This is the fourth step in the QAR instructional model. Or have kids pair up to ask each other their questions and practice answers before moving on to the next step, group work. And as always, if you can find a few moments, sit down next to a student and provide some quality one-on-one instruction.

Reading American History Informational Text

For the next lesson, Dorothy's eighth graders used the same grid sheet to record their QARs while reading an article on Martin Luther King, Jr., "Martin Luther King, Jr., Civil Rights Leader," to commemorate Dr. King's birthday. To facilitate their use of the QAR sheet, Dorothy instructed her students to first number each paragraph on the photocopied article and to refer to those numbers in their answers. The students were clearly making progress with QAR. Here's what they were able to do independently, which is the fifth step in the QAR instructional model:

- **Right There questions** (what I call "Right Here")

All students were able to compose Right Here questions, and this came as no surprise. These literal-level questions are not only the easiest to answer, they are also the easiest to generate.

- **Think and Search Questions** (what I call "Here and There")

For example, in her Here & There question box, Jane asked, "Who helped MLK, Jr."? She found her answer, "Rosa Parks, NAACP, SCLC, Robert Kennedy, and LBJ", in four different paragraphs. Dorothy believes that questions like these are the most important for students to be able to answer when reading nonfiction texts, because authors often provide information across multiple paragraphs, and readers are expected to pull together all that information in order to understand the overall concept. This is true not only in social studies, but in other content-area reading, as well.

- **Author and Me Questions**

Another student, Shinya, wrote in the Author and Me box: "Why do you think on MLK's grave it says, 'I'm free at last' "? Below the question, he wrote his answer: "He was free from all hate and racism." The quote on the tombstone comes from the text, but his answer comes from his head. Using the phrase "Why do you think," is a good way to begin this type of QAR.

For one of her A&M questions, Jane asked, "What do you think the SCLC does?" Her answer: "I think they meet and think of ideas to stop segregation." All the text stated was, "An organization called Southern Christian Leadership Conference (SCLC) was formed to continue the fight for civil rights." Jane had to mentally add meaning to that information in order to answer the question. Without this QAR activity, I wonder if she, or any of her classmates, would be aware of doing that. Of course, student questioning varies widely. One boy posed the question, "What is the Nobel Peace Prize?"

to the author because the answer was not provided in the text. The boy's answer was "A prize," which is a good example of a reader trying to construct meaning from a text that leaves him short. The important thing here is that he was able to identify information missing from the text and attempted to fill it in on his own. So his question was not a question for the author (A&M) but one to be answered by the reader alone (OMO).

On My Own Questions

On My Own questions require students to rely "solely on their prior knowledge to construct an answer," without referring to the text. Rachel's question "Would I stand up against racism?" shows that she is processing the content of the article beyond a literal level of information-gathering and taking it to the next level. Her answer, "Yes," while reassuring, prompted her teacher to request a more elaborate response: "Please explain."

In response to a paragraph about the assassination of Martin Luther King by James Earl Ray, Sydney asked this On My Own question: "Why did James Earl Ray shoot MLK, Jr.?" Below it she wrote, "Because he didn't agree with his ideas" which is a reasonable inference from the text, and we know that making inferences is a key reading comprehension skill.

Daniel's On My Own question, "Why would the woman call him a communist?" is actually an Author and Me question because the reader doesn't know who "the woman" is without reading the text. His classmate Hunter asked, "What is a communist?" an OMO question since it can be asked regardless of the text that was read and can be answered without reading it. Hunter couldn't answer it because he, and lots of other students, lacked the knowledge to do so.

When students attempt to answer OMO questions, they often realize that they cannot answer it on their own and look beyond the text to construct an answer. When a question entails looking to a new source, Taffy Raphael calls it a Think and Search with the search moving beyond the given text. I am always thrilled when students realize that sometimes they must seek out another source of information to answer a question.

USING QAR WITH GROUPS

Dorothy Syfert used this eight-step approach with groups working with QAR:

1. Number each paragraph in the reading selection. (For books, provide sticky note tabs.)

2. Have students read the selection independently and write their questions, answers, and paragraph numbers on the QAR Guide.

3. Divide students into groups of four or five and select one student to act as a facilitator by sharing his or her first Right Here question. Group members discuss the question to reach a consensus as to whether it's categorized correctly and accurately. Members take turns reading and discussing their Right Here questions.

4. Ask the facilitator to read a Here and There question and follow the same procedure described in the previous step. As time allows, repeat the same procedure for Author and Me and On My Own categories.

5. Have groups decide on the best question from each member and mark it with a star.

6. Invite facilitators to share the one or two best questions with the whole class. (The teacher could prompt by asking, "Which group had a best question in the Author and Me category?")

7. Have groups debrief with whole class on problems they faced and about any questions that had to be modified or recategorized.

8. Ask students to write a paragraph about the activity on the back of their grid. (Teacher could prompt students by suggesting they write about their favorite part of this activity, what was most difficult for their group, or ways that the activity could be improved.)

Reality Check

We were somewhat disappointed, but we were not shocked to find that some students were unable to generate questions in all categories. Kids learn at different rates, so it is to be expected that it will take some more time than others to gain proficiency with QAR. We must also remember that the ultimate goal here is not questioning for questioning's sake, or memorizing the different categories, but rather to build a key comprehension skill so that knowing when to ask a question eventually becomes second nature.

A few students didn't see the point of the QAR process. For example, Jane wrote, "I don't think [this helped my understanding] because I always think when I read." It might be that Jane in fact is already using some questioning framework in her mind as she reads. If so, wonderful! However, she may not actually be monitoring her understanding as she reads, and may only partially understand the text. The teacher must be the judge of this. Fortunately, we have many assessment options available to measure our students' comprehension of a reading assignment. These assessments can help a teacher determine whether a student like Jane has reached the independent application level.

If that is the case with Jane, then she is ready for an extension activity: preparation for a high-stakes reading test. As her teacher Dorothy pointed out, it is very useful to discern what types of questions are being asked on important standardized tests and to know where to go to find answers. Having advanced readers analyze sample exam questions through the QAR lens is a good example of differentiating our instruction.

Of course, in any classroom there are students who recognize the benefit of learning question types. Here are some quotes from some of Dorothy's eighth graders when prompted to reflect on whether QAR helped their understanding:

- Yes, because it made me have to think a lot about the story.

- A bit because I had to go back and find stuff to ask questions. The repetition helped. Every time you read you get better.

- Yes, because I think when you have to write your own questions, you have to think about it more than normal.

Thinking while reading. Now that's a good idea.

TIPS FOR TEACHING QAR TO MIDDLE GRADERS

1. **KEEP IT SIMPLE** Be sure not complicate QAR. Keep the categories clear, the practices focused, and the pacing slow but steady.

2. **OVER AND OVER** Always reiterate the reason for the questioning. Never assume everybody understands why you are assigning a question-asking activity. Assure your students that it's not just a cruel punishment; the purpose is to improve reading comprehension. Drive home the idea that successful readers constantly ask themselves questions as they read, and this method is a way to learn how to ask questions.

3. **BEFORE AND AFTER** Even with repetition of the mantra above, some kids won't buy in. Here's what Dorothy does to prove to her students that questioning supports comprehension. She has her students read a chapter independently and answer some questions afterward, serving as a pre-test. She then gives them five minutes to generate one or more H&T questions on their own. Then, in groups of three to five, students discuss the questions and answers. She then gives them new questions to answer in an independent post-test as a way of comparing the two approaches to reading.

4. **CUT A DEAL** Obviously some of the question categories are easier than others. Instead of requiring X number of questions for each question type, vary it by offering a choice, a package deal of a combination of types, or award more points for tackling tougher questions. Sometimes you can allow students to divide up the questions with a partner.

Sixth-Grade Language Arts: Using Children's Lit to Introduce QAR

Another colleague I collaborate with is Tom Cantwell, who teaches language arts/social studies to sixth graders at Cal Young Middle School in Eugene, Oregon. Tom quickly understood and appreciated the QAR method but cautioned that for his morning block, which includes a wide range of student reading ability, we should initiate QAR in the most simple and accessible way possible. So instead of starting with a story from a textbook, we decided to introduce QAR using a children's picture book.

I selected the story *Lizzie's Lion* by Dennis Lee (1983) because I've found that most middle graders have not read it, and the gruesome surprise ending is popular with them. I read them the story, stopping occasionally to ask my pre-established questions. I started with a few RHs, like "What kind of pet does Lizzy have?" and "How does Lizzy control her pet lion?" Then I asked an H&T, "Is this a real pet or an imaginary one?" Then I asked A&M questions, "Where is the robber? What happened to him?" and finally, an OMO: "Has anyone's house ever been robbed?" I had a total of 12 questions in the different categories.

For each question, the students and I quickly discussed the possible answers, which the class found engaging because the story was easily accessible even to the struggling readers. After I finished reading the story, each student was given a copy of my questions, with instructions to label each question type and write an answer. As always, I began by modeling exactly how to do these two steps. I used Reciprocal Teaching, labeling and answering the first question myself and then asking for a volunteer to label and answer question #2, and so on. By the fifth question they seemed ready to go solo (see Figure 3.1).

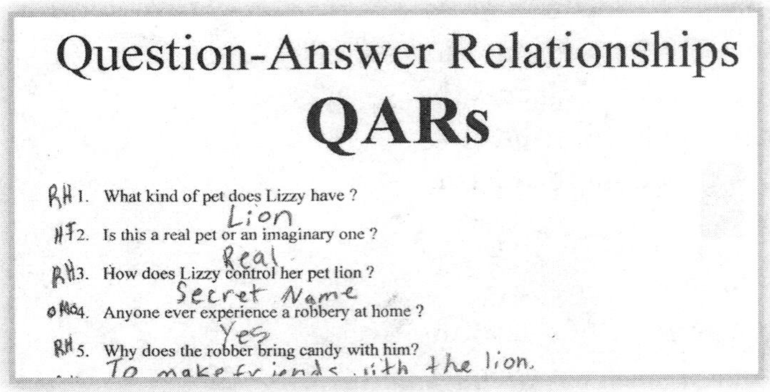

What Tom and I discovered upon reviewing the papers is that many students found it easier to answer the questions than to correctly label the question types. And, interestingly, some students labeled several questions with two QAR codes, which was either evidence of the student's uncertainty or that they couldn't distinguish between the two types. Either way, Tom and I weren't worried; the coding is only a vehicle for learning the far more important skill of questioning while reading. To nudge students toward generating their own questions, we provided them with a different practice sheet, using the question types as headers (see Figure 3.2). This format helped them to focus on the categories themselves.

Question-Answer Relationships
QARs

RH 1. What kind of pet does Lizzy have ?
    Lion
H&T 2. Is this a real pet or an imaginary one ?
    Real
RH 3. How does Lizzy control her pet lion ?
    Secret Name
OMO 4. Anyone ever experience a robbery at home ?
    Yes
RH 5. Why does the robber bring candy with him?
To make friends with the lion.

Figure 3.1 Student QARs for *Lizzy's Lions*

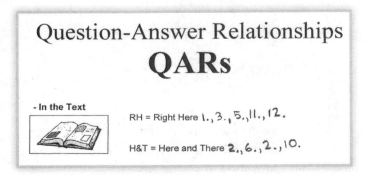

Question-Answer Relationships
QARs

- In the Text

RH = Right Here 1., 3., 5., 11., 12.

H&T = Here and There 2., 6., 2., 10.

Figure 3.2 Student QAR categories

QAR Plus

To move the class to a higher level of questioning, I added a third category at the bottom of the sheet entitled, "I Help the Author." This plants the seed for bringing the author into the questioning process. Copying Raphael's format, I subdivided this new category of questions in to two new ones:

I HELP THE AUTHOR	
QFA = Questions for the Author	**STA** = Suggestions to the Author
POSSIBLE QUESTION STARTERS:	**POSSIBLE SUGGESTION STARTERS:**
• Why did you decide to . . . • Did you ever consider . . . • What is the reason that you . . . • In my opinion, it would be better to . . . • How come you . . . • Instead of _____, you might consider . . . • When did you decide . . . • As an alternative to _____, why not . . .	• I think that you should . . . • Please allow me to suggest that . . . • Instead of _____, you might consider . . . • As an alternative to _____, why not . . .

I modeled two QtA questions: "Author, are you trying to scare little kids or do you think this will make them laugh?" and "Author, what age children did you write this story for?" (You'll notice that this is similar to activity as QtA in Chapter 2 on pages 44–48, but here it has a different format that fits with QAR.) Next I instructed the students to make up their own question and label it. One student asked the author, "Why a lion? Why not a transformer?" The second part of the question actually connects to the more challenging next category, Suggestions for the Author.

In response to "In Trouble," an excerpt from Gary Paulsen's *Woodsong* (1990), one student posed the following question to the author: "Did you ever actually race at Iditarod?" a reference to the famous dogsled race depicted in the story. Asking this kind of "I Help the Author" question helps students remember that reading is communication, a conversation between the author and the reader. Jeffery Wilhelm points out that reading is actually a partnership.

QAR With Poetry

Terry Kennedy, a teacher at Twin Peaks School in Tucson, Arizona, applied QAR Plus codes to poetry reading. She had her sixth graders try these questioning types on two Jack Prelutsky poems on Halloween, "The Bogeyman" and "The Vampire." (2003) Interestingly, they came up with far more suggestions than questions. Here are their suggestions for the poet (SfP):

- Describing how the Bogeyman looks would be more interesting.

- Describe where he lives.

- Make it scarier.

- Use more descriptive words.

- Make it rhyme.

The next suggestions are more specific, showing a deeper degree of feedback from student to writer:

- Put some of the Bogeyman's voice in the poem.

- Make the poem longer to describe the Bogeyman in more detail. For example, where he lives.

- Describe more of where he is waiting for you because it keeps saying he's "waiting for you."

- Have someone save the person before getting bitten by the vampire.

- I would suggest making someone kill the vampire at the end of the poem because they are evil. (Nice use of a starter phrase.)

The following Suggestions for the Poet begin by directly addressing the poet, showing readers' awareness of their audience:

- Mr. Prelutsky, very nice details but you need some more in the poem.

- Mr. Prelutsky, I suggest some easier to understand words.

- Mr. Prelutsky, I recommend some extra details and be more descriptive.

Terry surmises that her students were more inclined to make suggestions than to ask questions seeking clarification because of the genre of the reading assignment: poetry, as opposed to fiction or nonfiction. This may be a matter of familiarity. If the reader is unfamiliar with the content of a text with a genre like poetry, it can be difficult to self-monitor understanding through question-asking. We need to be aware of this as we work with our students on questioning.

Questioning the Author (QtA)

Questioning the Author (QtA) is a classic framework with a long track record of helping students improve their comprehension by self-monitoring as they read. Developed by reading researchers Isabel Beck and Margaret McKeown at the University of Pittsburgh's Learning Research and Development Center in 1997, QtA is based on reversing student attitudes toward reading by teaching them to recognize the potential "fallacy of the author." According to Beck and McKeown, readers ". . . tend to view text as basically comprehensible and authors as more or less infallible," so they often lose sight of the fact that the writer of the text is a player in the process.

I agree that most struggling readers blame themselves for the difficulties they encounter while reading. Many believe they are too slow, too confused, or just not smart enough to understand the text. Beck and McKeown dispute this notion. They maintain that no text is perfectly written; in fact, most leave quite a bit to be desired from a reader's standpoint. It is the reader's job to work at making sense of the text. The intent is not to make our students overly critical or negative, but rather to help readers perceive a reading assignment as created by another human being who may or may not have fully succeeded at communicating his or her intended message.

Beck and McKeown use a superb simile: "Readers are like sheep that an author is trying to herd in a particular direction. If there is a hole in the fence, the sheep are sure to find it and go astray. . . QtA is dedicated to preventing our student readers from going through these holes." Many school reading resources are riddled with such "holes in the fence." To train students to approach reading with a careful eye on the author, QtA is a collaborative process. It works like this: The teacher leads a group of students through a reading passage, stopping periodically at key spots to ask an open-ended question called a query that causes the reader to scrutinize the meaning of the author's words. Queries differ from traditional teacher questions, which have definite answers. While Beck and McKeown approve of asking recall type questions in some situations—such as to confirm literal-level understanding—they are more interested in pushing readers deeper into the reading.

Questioning the Author has had a major impact on my teaching, influencing me to emphasize the importance of taking a critical stance as a reader and not just focusing on recalling information. I have applied the strategy with middle graders using both fiction and nonfiction, and I have found that students appreciate partnering with the author to make sense of the reading instead of going it alone. Young readers take to this approach quite naturally and even eagerly. It is different, and different is good. It is empowering for students to see that their problems in comprehension may actually be due to the author's limitations and not their own. This notion keeps them on their toes when they are reading.

I have experimented with advancing the QtA technique from teacher queries to student-initiated queries to help middle-grade students as they make the transition to becoming more independent, adult-like readers. Putting kids in the driver's seat is a large jump, of course, and Professor Beck cautioned me not try it until students were experienced in the QtA method.

Science Students Question Their Textbook

In a seventh-grade science class, I partnered with Angie Ruzicka, a highly motivating science teacher who focuses on reading strategies to support her students' quest to make meaning of the concepts in the class textbook. For years, Angie has recognized that she cannot assume her students enter her classes with grade-level reading comprehension; rather, like all content-area teachers, she needs to include reading instruction in concert with her content instruction to support the below grade-level readers.

We began piloting the QtA approach with a group of six seventh graders whom Angie selected for their interest in science and wide range of reading ability. Over a period of two months, in an available nearby classroom, I spent five class periods training this group.

In our first meeting, I said, "I'm going to teach you a new way of reading that will help you to better understand the next chapter in your science book." I was tempted to tell them that we would be, jointly "constructing a coherent representation of the text," as Beck and McKeown put it, but I refrained. Instead, I said, "Our goal as readers is help each other figure out what Henry Milne, the lead author of your textbook, is trying to teach us."

Segments and Queries

I led the group through an introductory QtA session on a chapter called "Microscope Pioneers." Prior to class, I read the chapter and found 11 key places where we would pause to discuss the meaning and check for understanding. Each segment contained either an idea that was essential for students to understand or a potential trouble spot that struck me as likely to cause confusion. Segments could be one paragraph or several, or just a single sentence.

I began with a teacher query, which Beck and McKeown describe as "general probes… [that] encourage young readers to take notice of a text [and] consider meaning and develop ideas, not just passively receive and retrieve information." Here are some that I came up with for different segments of the chapter:

- What does our author Henry really want us to know so far?

- I wonder why the author included this part here.

- That's weird. What do you think the author meant by this sentence?

- Could the author have stated this idea better, using different words?

Notice that each of my queries refers to the author, and each one sets off a mini-discussion of the segment, stimulating active thinking about the content. The queries led to an animated and interesting conversation about the inventors of microscopes. I think this occurred because the queries put us on a mutual quest for understanding, as opposed to me playing the traditional teacher role of the Great Inquisitor trying to test their comprehension or even catch them failing to comprehend. Beck and McKeown describe the "role of teacher [changing] from a quiz show host to a discussion facilitator."

Huge difference. It was fun, it was collegial, and it was effective in helping them learn what they were supposed to learn from the book.

Angie commented later that queries sometimes serve to expose an author's errors, misstatements, or omissions.

Teacher Queries

Queries have several functions. They can:

- highlight key points that students must understand, as well as potential trouble spots

- help students get a handle on a text

- make the text comprehensible

- facilitate group discussion about an author's ideas

- guide students to recognize the difference between what an author says and what he or she means beyond the author's words to his or her message

And here's a helpful tip: Queries should be phrased in students' language.

A few weeks later, I used the same approach for another chapter, "Exploring Cells." This time, though, I photocopied the chapter with the bracketed segments and queries I had inserted, so each student could see what I had done to prepare for our Questioning the Author lesson (see Figure 3.3). By making the procedure *transparent* to the student-readers, I was planting the seed for them to eventually take over. The ultimate goal of any questioning method, of course, is the ability for students to *internalize* question-asking to become better, more independent readers.

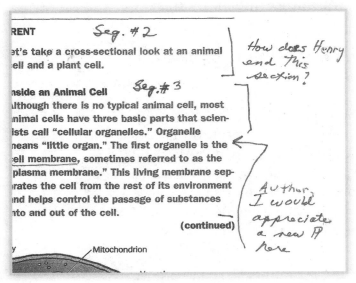

Figure 3.3 A sample of a teacher's segments and queries

Students Take Over

Next, we tackled segmenting a chapter called "The Nutritional Needs of Plants." I began by reading the first paragraph to them as they followed along. I asked the kids to decide if the paragraph was totally clear or if not, to identify any confusing information. We agreed to mark off any confusing parts as individual segments or to break it down further. If the paragraph was clear, I read the next one to see if it belonged with the first and to determine if students found it confusing. At one point, group member named Kade suggested that a segment is "a part of a section that is different" from the rest of the text—a good, student-friendly definition.

I modeled how to ask a query about the segment, and I instructed students to write their queries at the end of the segment on their copies of the chapter. We worked our way through the three pages of text delineating segments, generating queries, and discussing possible answers. The teacher's role is to be the more experienced reader who guides younger readers, in the words of Beck and McKeown, "to crack open a text's meaning." Beck and McKeown refer to this as "interspersed reading," where we teach students to approach a text little by little, idea by idea, to tease out what an author is intending to tell them. In response to this method, one student, Mitchell, asked "Why doesn't the author *just come out and tell us* that?"

As we progressed through the chapter, I noticed that the students were becoming increasingly comfortable admitting their own confusions about the text. I can think of two reasons for this. First, I showed no hesitancy in admitting when I was confused, and also, we kept referring to the author and speculating what he would have to say in response to our queries. The kids liked how this takes some of the pressure off them as readers. Beck and McKeown explain it this way: "Meanings and explanations emerged from several sources, not from the students alone, not from the teacher alone, not from the text, but a collaboration that involved all three."

The students recognized that this was a very different way of reading their science book. Their teacher agreed. After watching the videotape I made of the group, Angie used a great metaphor to describe to me what she saw her students doing: They were *reading detectives* using the author's clues as evidence to establish a case, i.e., a case for what they comprehended.

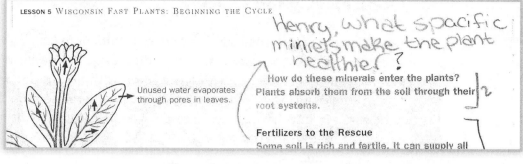

Figures 3.4 Ashley's query to the author

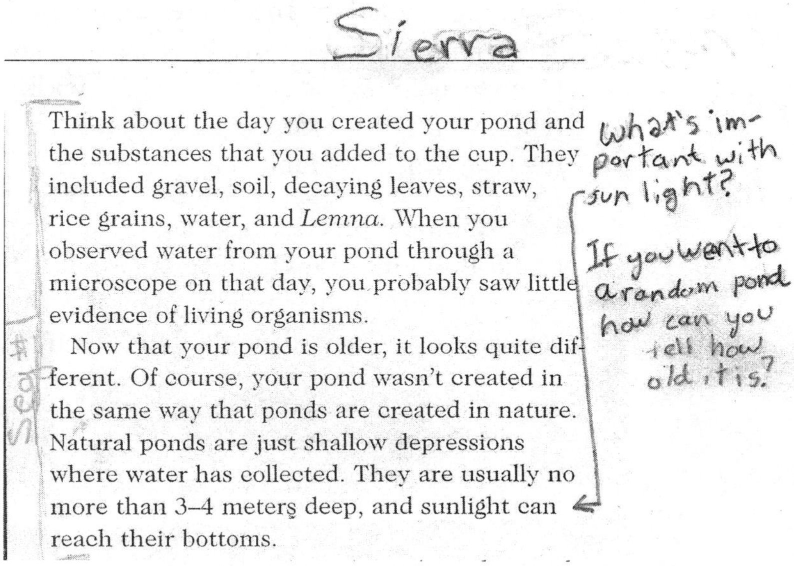

Figures 3.5 Sierra's queries

She was pleased with the "different spirit" she witnessed, an esprit de corps that boosted reading comprehension and reading confidence.

In the next session, we co-generated segments and queries for the first page of a chapter called "The Changing Pond." This gently moved the students in the direction of more independence. Next, I released them to try it with partners on the second page. Toward the end of the chapter, I asked them to segment and query independently (see figures 3.4 and 3.5). The kids did a great job. They seemed to get the method, and I was confident they were ready to teach their classmates the QtA technique.

Oops: Moving Too Quickly

The following week, Angie and I asked each student to lead a group of five classmates in reading the next assigned chapter. It did not go very well. While some them were partially able to conduct a QtA conversation with their peers, most struggled at least some of the time. I was guilty of rushing the process and for not heeding Beck's advice to be sure students have plenty of teacher-led experience with the method before expecting them to teach this technique. The key is that the transition to student queries must be *gradual*.

The question cadre and I regrouped the next day, and I apologized for putting them in a tough situation. They weren't upset or even uncomfortable about the experience. They thought it went okay, but they had suggestions for doing it better. We discussed when to ask a review question, when to ask a more open-ended query, and when both types would be useful. One group member, Mitchell wanted to ask a combination of the two, which we dubbed a "questry."

For additional practice, I brought along a great supplemental article I found online titled "Building Your Own Watergarden: Steps for Constructing a New Pond," and the students worked their way through it with an eye toward how they would teach it to someone else. They segmented the text into passages, generated queries about important or confusing parts, and highlighted key information from the author (see Figure 3.6). In short, they dissected the text, and more important, they understood the purpose of the activity: to improve their comprehension of the text.

What I discovered during this lesson, besides how much practice middle graders need in order to learn the QtA method, was how motivated the students are to get answers from the author. Speculating on the author's intended meaning was fine, but they really wanted to know for sure. Perhaps hearing me routinely refer to their textbook's author by name inspired them to direct their own queries to the author of the Web article.

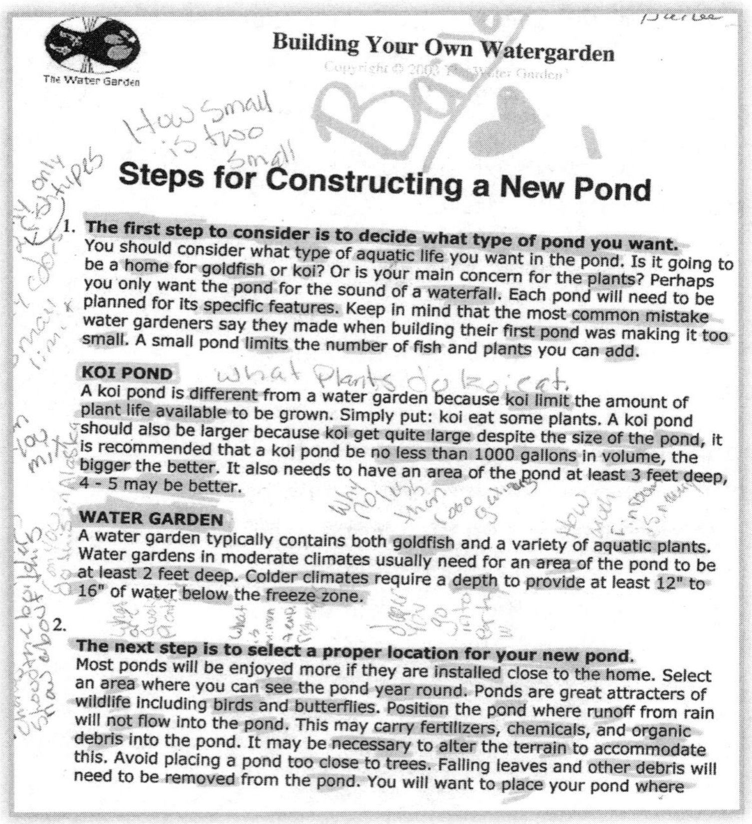

Figure 3.6 Bailee's segments and queries

Literally Questioning the Author—
With a Postage Stamp

Next, it was Angie's turn to use QtA to guide her whole class through a chapter in their science book on the dangers of anabolic steroids. She segmented it and posed queries for a whole-class reading and discussion. You will notice she refers to the author in her queries as a way to get her students to keep in mind the person responsible for writing the chapter (see Figure 3.7).

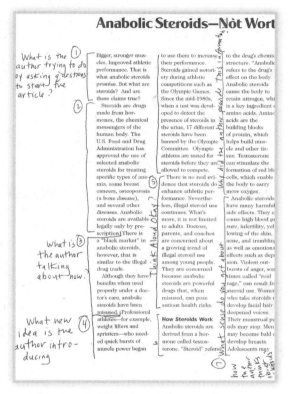

Figure 3.7 A science teacher's segments and queries

After her students understood the role of queries in supporting reading comprehension, Angie had them generate their own queries to the author as they read a chapter titled "Life in the Bone Zone" (see Figure 3.8). To assist them, I provided each student with a set of five Query Starters. The lead author's name was easily identified on the title page of the book, and I decided to include it in some of the Query Starters:

- Mr. Milne, are you saying that. . . ?
- Do you expect me to. . .
- Mr. Milne, I don't understand. . .
- What do you mean by. . .
- Mr. Milne, why do you. . .

Figure 3.8 Students using query starters to write questions

Angie decided to use 4" x 6" index cards for students to record their queries because she knew that the textbook would be undergoing a revision, and she wanted her students to send their queries in the form of a postcard to the author. Here are two postcards addressed to the author with a query for the three boldface sections of the chapter (see Figure 3.9).

The class generated many interesting questions to the author:

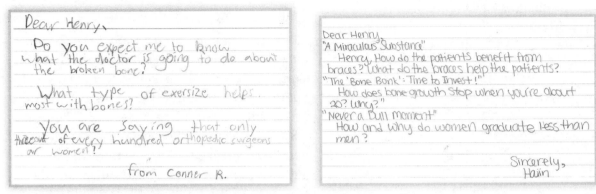

Figure 3.9 Conner and Hain's questions to the author

- ◉ Kelsey wrote, "I don't understand how to fix the broken bone on page 155."

- ◉ Mitchell stated, "I don't understand what *kindled* means. How come you don't make it easier for us to understand? I do like how it's a different word, but could you please make a key?"

- ◉ Emily asked, "Are you saying that you have to drink milk because of building stronger bones? Do I have to have milk or [other] calcium products?"

- ◉ Laura inquired, "What do you mean by she 'fixes the bones?' Only a select few of us that have had them 'fixed' know what happens."

- ◉ Josh asked, "What do you mean by 'bone is the most miraculous substance'?"

- ◉ And the most common question: "Why are you saying that only three out of every 100 orthopedic surgeons are women?"

One boy added, "Isn't that just coincidence?" (No girls did, however.)

- And good news from Bailee (a member of my trained cadre): "I totally understand the section 'Never a Dull Moment!' "

Some students did not need any of my query starters. I like the following ones, which they invented on their own, seeking additional information:

- Genie wanted to know, "What's the difference between fracture and breaks? You use both and I'm confused."

- Ashley needed clarification, "What is a medical journal? Is it like a regular Journal? Explain :)"

- Cooper asked, "What if somebody is lactose intolerant and [also] is allergic to soybeans and stuff? Then what do they do [for calcium]?"

- Laura wrote: "It would help if there were more details, and what you do, or how long it takes to recover [from a fracture]."

- Here's one more excellent question: "Along with exercise and a healthy diet, what can you do to strengthen your bone bank?"

These student-generated queries to the author are personal comprehension guideposts. They enable students, the teacher, and the author (when he receives postcards) to track the students' understanding. From about 30 students in each of her three science classes, Angie collected well over 300 questions to the author. Some were repeated, of course, but the number is impressive. This is a very worthwhile activity for three important reasons:

1. **It proves that students can think and read at the same time by generating questions while reading. What a relief!**

2. **It offers teachers a window into their students' level of reading comprehension before test time, when it's too late.**

3. **It provides useful feedback to the author of the book: How are my explanations of scientific principles playing out in real classrooms?**

Figure 3.10 Students gathering postcards to mail to the author

To sweeten the assignment, Angie addressed a large envelope to the author, and after a quick proofreading of the postcards, students put their notes in the envelope to be mailed (see Figure 3.10).

Sorting the Questions

Before mailing their postcards to the author, Angie and I categorized them into different types of questions. While this is not necessary in the QtA framework, I was curious to see if different readers were tracking their reading at different degrees of complexity. Additionally, Angie was sensitive about not overloading the author with too many questions. I volunteered to type a list of the most common questions and include them in the envelope. Here are some good ones in both categories.

1. Puzzlement questions, which I modified from Ciardiello's original framework, reveal basic gaps in understanding:

> Elsie: "What does *orthopedic* mean?"

Even though the author provided a major context clue—"Dr. Tosi is a pediatric orthopedic surgeon. In other words, she fixes children's bones"—the doctor's three-word medical title was too complicated for Elsie.

> Devan: "Henry, I don't understand, what kind of things could someone do to break their bones?"

Puzzlement questions, you will recall from Ciardiello, also arise when a reader perceives incoming information as contradictory to what he or she believes. The following questions reveal puzzlement over the author's use of the term "bone bank."

> Nathan: What is your bone bank? Where is it?

> Alli: Do a lot of people donate bone or bone marrow to bone banks?

The term clearly isn't familiar to these readers. Instead of comprehension, the readers experienced confusion.

2. Wonderment questions seek more from the author. They reveal a desire for supporting information, a pondering of possibilities, an extension beyond the basic facts of the reading. Wonderments are aroused by curiosity. Even though none of these questions begin with *I wonder why,* some students zoomed in on the chapter's section on bone breaks:

- Sabrina: What bone is the worst bone to break? And what is an unusual bone to break or fracture?

- Jimmy: What is the worst bone injury recorded?

Other readers wanted more details about women doctors:

- Paige: Exactly how many women orthopedic surgeons are there?

- Sophia: Has the number of women working in this profession increased since 2000 since this was published?

- Jimmy, who was pondering a future career, wanted to know: If I want to be a pediatric orthopedic surgeon, what's a good school to go to?

- And his follow-up: How much does a pediatric orthopedic surgeon get paid?

Pretty impressive questioning, especially considering that neither Angie nor I are experts teaching QtA. Angie mailed the questions to the author, but unfortunately he is retiring from the textbook team. Bad timing! But in his reply, he promised he would pass them on to the person working on the book's revisions.

Students Learn How to Question a Literature Author

In Chapter 2, I described how Tom Cantwell's sixth-grade language arts students read *The Whale Rider* and generated four different types of questions (see page 44). Using notebook paper divided into four sections, students recorded questions as they read. The fourth category, Questions to the Author, is where students address their questions, confusions, and concerns directly to the person who wrote the novel.

Here, a student asks the author a few questions that reveal a fuzzy understanding of certain aspects of the book (see Figure 3.11).

Drew's QtAs were:

- Are there still fairies?
- Why does the nana not like the phone?

Sorry, No Postcards This Time

At this point, Tom and I considered having his class carefully copy their questions onto a postcard, a memo format, or a longer letter to the author. But he chose not to.

Why not? Time ran out, and he had to move on. The questions remained in rough draft form and did not leave the classroom. Of course, it would have very exciting for the students to experience writing to a published author, and thrilling if the author had written back, but we cannot pull this off every time we assign reading. And we shouldn't feel guilty about it. Tom certainly did not; his kids had a successful and rewarding reading experience with the novel.

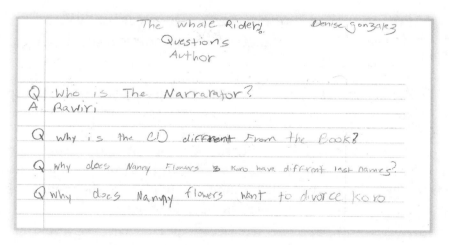

Figure 3.11 Questions to the author of *The Whale Rider*

Summary

Like QAR, QtA is a powerful questioning framework that has stood the test of time. These approaches have taught me much about student questioning, and they have inspired me to continue to experiment with and implement other questioning activities.

QtA is very powerful way of altering students' perceptions of what reading comprehension actually is. It levels the playing field for struggling readers by convincing them that comprehension is a two-way street, and that they must work together with the author must in order to achieve understanding. With effective teacher modeling and lots of practice, middle graders can learn how to take over from their teacher and independently query the author to support their comprehension.

QtA and QAR can be incorporated into reading instruction after students have practiced some of the starter activities in Chapter 1 and intermediate activities in Chapter 2. To me, it makes sense to ease into question-asking, but if you feel ready, it would certainly be appropriate to start earlier in the year or semester. Many teachers have. Finally, keep in mind that neither approach should be superficially presented to students with the hope that they will be quickly mastered. Both require some time to learn.

CHAPTER 4

Advanced Questioning Activities

○ Why did you have Mia's reaction to Mango so strong, if you were just going to have him die?

○ Did you feel it was necessary to do that to Mia when she already had problems in her life?

~ *Mikella, a seventh grader, posing a "Type III" question*
to the author of the novel A Mango-Shaped Space
about the role of the protagonist's pet cat

The advanced questioning activities in this chapter build upon the activities presented in the preceding chapters. You will see a direct connection to previous questioning activities, and you will recognize possibilities for inclusion into your own teaching. Some of your students may be ready for these advanced activities, and I will help you adapt them into something that will work for your whole class.

A PASS Approach

But first, a road marker. I see our approach thus far as following the first three steps in a "PASS" approach to reading comprehension:

Passive = Too many of our students are *passive* readers: mentally inactive and, therefore, disengaged.

Alert = We need to teach them how to ask questions when they read to transform them into *alert* readers.

SideKick = We need to help them become *sidekicks* to the author through congenial, helpful questioning.

Suspicious = We need to teach readers to take a skeptical, critical, *suspicious* stance in queries to the author to aid in their comprehension.

Now we are ready for that last step: teaching students to be suspicious readers. Suspicious reading takes students to the highest level of questioning—critical comprehension—by teaching them to ask tough questions about the author's purpose, position, decisions, bias, or agenda.

Creating Suspicious Readers

As a veteran adult reader, I admit that when I read an article in the newspaper, a magazine or journal, or online, my stance is suspicious. I carefully read to see if:

- the author has a *point of view*—what position is he or she promoting?

- the author has a *bias*—if so, is it hidden or plainly visible?

- the author has a *background*—who is this person; what else has she written?

- the author has an *assumption*—what is the basis of his point of view?

- the author is *overstating* some things—if so, why the exaggeration?

- the author is *understating*, forgetting, or ignoring some things—if so, why the oversight or avoidance?

- the author is using *rhetorical devices*—are they masking anything?

And most important,

- Do I agree or disagree, appreciate or resent, the writing?

- Do I feel energized or bored by it?

In short, I read with my hands on my hips, my eyes narrowed, and my brain on alert. This critical attitude puts me on the lookout not only for what the author is telling me, but what the author is not telling me, plus possible reasons for both. I do this mainly when reading nonfiction, but I can assume this stance when reading fiction, too, especially when the author is not engaging me as much I feel I deserve to be.

But this stance does not only scrutinize the author's intentions; it simultaneously scrutinizes the author's ideas—just like Mikella did in the questions quoted at the top of this chapter. This suspicious approach to reading moves a reader up a notch on the Thinking Skills Hierarchy to critical analysis, synthesis of ideas, and careful evaluation. Nod your head if you would like more of this type of thinking in your classroom. If I were king for a day, my first decree would be to elevate all readers, students and adults alike, to this level of critical reading. Since I am not so ordained, let's explore questioning activities that guide students to this high level of reading.

Bloom's Taxonomy of Thinking

If you feel that your students are ready for this advanced questioning activity, or if you feel that they are close enough to try it, here is a helpful structure to assist you in moving them forward: Bloom's Hierarchy. There are Type I, II, III questions in Bloom's Taxonomy of Thinking (1956), and each question type increases the cognitive demand on the reader.

- Type I questions seek to *understand* and *comprehend* information in the reading.

- Type II questions cause the reader to *analyze, critically examine,* and *appraise* the stated information by recognizing what is missing, not stated, or only implied.

- Type III questions *judge* the author's position (*evaluation*) and/ or *formulate* an alternative, or even contrary, *hypothesis* (*synthesis*)

The italicized words come from Diane Heacox's "Challenge Levels" in her outstanding book *Differentiating the Regular Classroom: How to Read and Teach All Learners, Grades 3–12* (2002).

The idea of connecting types of questions to Bloom comes from my friend and former teaching colleague, Howard Yank, of the Vancouver, Washington School District. His district uses the term "cognitive demand" to identify what the learner needs to do at each level. You will notice some overlap—and some differences—between Bloom's terminology and my three question types, as well as Raphael's QARs.

- Level One (Literal Questions): The answer is *right there* in the text. The words used to make up the question are often *the same words* that are in the answer.

- Level Two (Inferential Questions) The answer is in the text, but it needs to be put together with different pieces of information from the book. You have to think and search for the answer.

- Level Two (Interpretive Questions) You need to think about what you know and what the author has said in the text. The answer will be from both the author and you as you infer meaning. The answer won't be found on the printed page, but the information to answer the question is there.

- Level Three (Bigger-Picture Questions) The question is asking for your own thoughts about an issue or theme related to the text. It can be creative or open-ended and there is no right or wrong answer, but the answer should be supported by the text and your personal experiences and beliefs.

You will notice in this framework that type II questions are subdivided into two types: IIA Inferential, in which the answer is provided by the author somewhere across parts of the text, and IIB Interpretative, derived from a combination of information from the author and the reader. The cognitive demand on the students increases with each question type.

Three Types of Questions in High School

Bart Pollard, a literature teacher at Cottage Grove High School in Cottage Grove, Oregon, uses Three Types of Questions in his College Prep Lit class. Bart had his students individually read and generate questions for one of three scholarly articles he provided about Edgar Allan Poe. Then he placed students into temporary small groups of three or four based on which of the three articles they read. The groups were told to discuss their article by asking group members Type I, II, and III questions.

This group questioning activity connects back to the earlier one called QtM, QtC, QtT, QtA (see Chapter 2). We now add a fifth audience—peers—to the mix. Thus,

Questions to My Peers, or QtP. To add structure to this cooperative group discussion, we could use the format created by Harvey Daniels in his classic book *Literature Circles* (2002). Daniels identifies various roles for group members to play, including a passage picker, vocabulary enricher, and discussion director who develops questions for the group to discuss.

I have had success using a worksheet developed in the Vancouver, Washington School District to assist students in generating discussion questions for a literature assignment. It nicely incorporates the levels of questions, and also provides useful starter phrases for each level of questions (see page 105). The one modification I recommend is that instead of the discussion director being the sole generator of questions, have *all* the group members generate questions and submit them to the discussion director, whose job becomes prioritizing and picking the best ones to use with the group.

Prompts to Assist Student Challenge Questions

Providing students with prompts like those on page 105 is a good strategy. They are not intended to elicit formulaic questions, but rather to help students learn how to generate questions at increasingly complex levels. These prompts also demonstrate a respectful yet assertive tone of voice for students. Here is an additional set of prompts I developed for Type III questions:

- You say . . ., but what about . . . ?
- You imply. . ., but . . . ?
- Are you saying that. . . ? If so, . . . ?
- Are you suggesting that . . . ?
- Why don't you mention . . . ?
- Aren't you overlooking . . . ?
- Did you forget about . . . ?
- Didn't you consider . . . ?
- If what you say is true, what about . . . ?
- What you say is interesting, but I think that . . .
- How can you believe . . . when . . . ?
- With all due respect, shouldn't you . . . ?

I and Level II questions to avoid overloading anybody on his or her first try. David instructed his students to read a chapter in their world cultures textbook, and then create a Level I and a Level II question to go along with the information under each of 18 subheadings. For support, he provided these definitions and examples:

> A Level I question is a straightforward question with an answer straight from the book. An example of a Level I would be: *What did Mao rename China after the Communists took over?* Answer: *The People's Republic of China.*

> A Level II question requires more thought and may not be stated directly in the book. An example of a Level II would be: *What does it mean for China to be named a Republic?* Answer: *It means that now the people have a say in who will be in the government because in a republic people have the right to vote.*

Here is a Level I question that a student came up with for a section of the chapter called "Creating a New Order."

> ⊙ "Why did the communists turn China into a totalitarian state?" Her answer came directly from the book: "To resolve order and achieve their revolutionary goals."

In the next section of the assigned reading, she asks a Level II:

> ⊙ "Would Mao still be in leadership if the Communist Party chose [from] two leaders for election?" Her answer— "Maybe he would not have been chosen… because [other] people now have two leaders to choose from"—shows that she is bringing in additional information from her knowledge of the world in order to answer the question.

Brittany, a college-prep student, asked this Level II question for the same section on Mao's leadership:

> ⊙ "How do you think propaganda made Mao a hero?"

Beginning with a great Type II question starter—"How do you think"—Brittany wrote an answer that shows that she was thinking beyond the information found in the text: "Propaganda helped Mao become a hero because it helped China know more about him, and it helped spread his intentions. The communists also only advertised the good things about Mao and made him appealing to the Chinese people." Note how Brittany's use of precise vocabulary supports her thinking.

Carolina used the same starter phrase as Brittany to generate this Type II question for a different section:

> "Do you think The Great Leap Forward was the brightest idea to propose and follow through on?" Her answer: "I think Mao shouldn't have proposed it, nor actually gone through with it because trying to do what's best for the country takes time. When you want something to come out right, it takes time and not done fast or sloppily." Carolina is beyond literal-level comprehension; she is into interpretation and evaluation of the material.

Andy used another helpful question starter for his Type II question:

> "Compare and contrast what the government was supposed to be, and what it was in reality." Andy is acting as the teacher by posing an essay-type question. This reveals advanced thinking.

Andy and Carolina appear to be ready for Type III questions, but not all of their classmates are, so David opted to hold off introducing the third type of question. If you believe your class will be more successful with I and II, go with your gut feeling and play it safe. You can add Type III whenever you think they're ready. When teachers adapt lessons to best fit their students' abilities and needs, the chances for student success go way up. But what about using these question types with middle-grade learners?

Three Types of Questions in Middle School

Middle-grade readers can also use the three type of questions. They have already had some experience posing questions to the author, although not quite as pointedly as Type III.

Middle School Readers Challenge the Author of a Novel

Jeff Wyman teaches a course called "Book Club" to seventh and eighth grade students in a bilingual French language immersion program at Roosevelt Middle School in Eugene, Oregon. Since kindergarten, these kids have spent half of their school day being instructed in French. Jeff speaks and teaches on the English side, so it was his job to teach 35 of them how to read fiction critically and how to discuss, reflect, and write about it in English. Their current reading assignment was the novel *A Mango-Shaped Space* (2003) by Wendy Mass, about a girl with a rare neurological condition called synesthesia in which senses are heightened and "crossed."

I asked Jeff how the Three Types of Questions activity could be modified for middle schoolers. Jeff suggested that we keep it the same, except to substitute the terms "Thin, Thick, and Thickest" for "Type I, II, and III." He timed the activity to coincide with the second-to-last chapter of the novel. My job was to introduce the kids to the three levels of question-asking. No problem, Jeff assured me, because this class was very advanced in terms of intellectual curiosity, cooperation, and self-directed learning. The students came from a solid elementary school program that instilled hard work, academic seriousness, and the importance of learning, and their middle school program fostered higher standards of excellence.

Jeff was right; it *was* easy. I simply told the class that I, too, was reading the same novel, and that while reading it, I couldn't stop asking questions. "Same with your teacher," I said, "It's a habit with us." I shared a few of our questions by writing them on the board and distributing a companion worksheet to each student.

- What is Mia's history project about? (I had put the book down for a week, and I confessed that I couldn't remember.)

- What happened to Mango? (My wife also was interested in reading the book, and she was a bit concerned about the cat.)

- Why do adolescent girls respond so much more passionately to the death of a pet compared to a death of a human? (This was Jeff's question, and surprisingly, most of the girls agreed, plus they offered various explanations.)

- Why did you (author Wendy Mass) decide that the cat needed to die? What advantage to your plot did it provide? (I tend to object to obvious, predictable events in young-adult fiction.)

- What is the primary purpose of Jenna? Is she important to Mia as a friend, or is she important to your story because her mother is deceased? (Jeff and I really couldn't tell about this character.)

Next, I pointed out that these questions cover a range of complexity. Some are quite easy to answer by reviewing the text, some require supplementing information from an outside source, and some are unanswerable without more information from the author. I instructed the students to rank these questions by degree of difficulty, from easiest to most difficult.

As they set about their task, the students quickly recognized that the first two were the easy questions, the third was more difficult, and the last two were the hardest to answer. Then I provided them with a copy of the definitions, purposes, and point values of the types of questions:

- **Thin =** answerable right in the text; helpful for review of important information; worth one point. (Jeff added that Thin questions cannot be too thin, like: "What is the main character's name?")
- **Thick =** possibly answerable by seeking outside, supplemental information, either from prior knowledge or from another source; useful for deeper processing of the information; worth two points.
- **Thickest =** not definitively answerable, but probing, open-ended, critical; essential for getting to the heart of, and for challenging, the author's message; worth three points.

Jeff instructed the class to take 15 minutes to generate three questions from their reading, totaling seven points. He told them that they could choose which types of questions to ask, but they needed to use more than one category. Afterward, he would multiply their scores by three to make the assignment worth a total of 21 points.

Right away a student asked, "Can we write more questions than just three?" Jeff looked at me, and we both nodded and grinned simultaneously.

"Sure," he said. "Go for it. Just be sure to label your questions with the correct point value." Many kids quickly decided to open their books and review the chapters to help them think of questions. The atmosphere in the room became quiet, focused, industrious. Every student generated interesting questions, and all categories were represented.

Shaeda decided to earn her seven points by asking one Thickest and two Thick questions (see Figure 4.1).

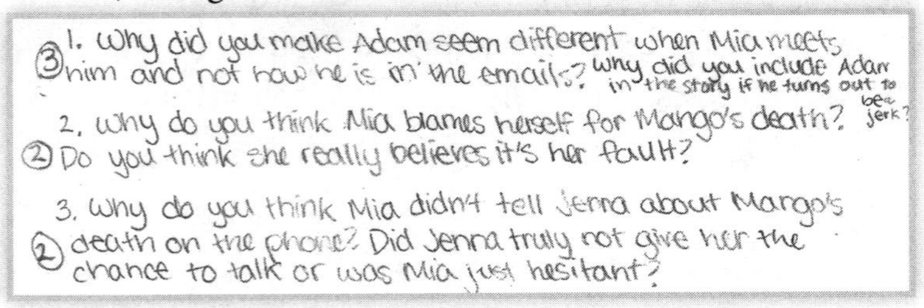
③ 1. Why did you make Adam seem different when Mia meets him and not how he is in the emails? Why did you include Adam in the story if he turns out to be a jerk?

② 2. Why do you think Mia blames herself for Mango's death? Do you think she really believes it's her fault?

② 3. Why do you think Mia didn't tell Jenna about Mango's death on the phone? Did Jenna truly not give her the chance to talk or was Mia just hesitant?

Figure 4.1 Shaeda's questions about *A Mango-Shaped Space*

Coincidentally, the principal happened to enter the classroom, and ended up staying to watch what was going on. What was going on was reading comprehension, critical thinking, and intellectual curiosity. Truly a beautiful experience for me as the visiting teacher.

Procedure for Training Students With Three Types of Questions

1. Refer students back to a reading assignment recently completed. Select a passage of a few paragraphs.

2. Tell them they will be asking three questions while they review the passage: a Type I, Type II, and Type III question.

3. Ask students if anyone wants to predict the differences among the types.

4. Explain the definitions (see page 110).

5. Model how to ask a Type I Question; ask if anyone can think up another one.

6. Model how to ask a Type II Question; ask if anyone can think up another one.

7. Model how to ask a Type III Question; ask if anyone can think up another one.

8. Provide students with copies of a short reading assignment—a few paragraphs to one page in length.

9. Provide students with three different colored pencils and tell students to:

   - Underline the text for an answer to a Type I Question they invent on their own using the _____ colored pencil; nearby they write the question with the same color.

   - Underline the text for an answer to a Type II Question they invent on their own using the _____ colored pencil; nearby they write the question with the same color.

   - Underline the text for an answer to a Type III Question they invent on their own using the _____ colored pencil; nearby they write the question with the same color.

POSSIBLE MODIFICATIONS

○ Use an overhead transparency of the text passage to model the types. Underline the answers using three different colored overhead pens. Then write in the questions nearby using the same colors.

○ Instead of photocopying the text and providing colored pencils or using the overhead projector, have students work directly in their textbooks (or lit anthologies). Select a short passage to work on and lead them through it by modeling the different types of questions. As you guide them, they copy the questions onto a folded three-columned paper. When you think they get the difference among the types, turn them loose to continue on their own or with a partner.

○ Instead of addressing all three types at once, start with Type I or maybe Types I and II, and save Type III for another time.

Sharing in Literature Circles

Next, kids relocated into their literature circle groups, and the discussion directors called on volunteers to share their best questions in each category and discuss them together. As Jeff and I circulated and sat in with the groups, we found the level of discussion, reflection, and cooperation so impressive that we felt we were part of a book group of adult readers. The questions, the give and take, and the level of maturity we witnessed was truly something to see. Because they already knew the lit circle routine, and because they took responsibility for their own learning, the students required no intervention from us. Jeff and I participated as equals.

Sharing With the Whole Class

The final step was to debrief as a whole class. The students returned to their desks, and I asked who wanted to share a good one-pointer. Not many volunteers, but when I asked for Thick questions, they offered plenty of good ones.

- Madeleine: "What do you think it would feel like to be Mia knowing Billy's mother doesn't want you around?"

- Taylor: "Do you think Mia was cheating on her math tests, or did she just figure out a creative way to solve them?"

- Sam: "If you had synesthesia, would you try harder in math or cheat like Mia?"

- Krissy: "When Mia walked into the room where the meeting was being held, she becomes very nervous. How do you think you would feel if you had to do that too?"

- Megan: "Will Billy ever find out he has synesthesia? Will his mom ever consider contacting Mia in the future when Billy's colors don't stop, or do you think he has been making this up all along?"

- Celine: "Mia thinks that she is responsible for Mango's death because she forgot to give him his pill and left him outside. Is it really her fault?"

- Sarah: "Why did Jenna and Mia have such an uptight relationship when they were best friends?"

- Natalie: "What do you think happened between Mia and Adam? Was it because Adam was focused on kissing Mia that he didn't have any sympathy for her cat's death?"

- Braeden: "People say that when you are hurt badly, you lose something. Mia lost her synesthesia gift, her cat, and all the memories of her grandfather. How will she ever regain herself and become strong again?"

After collecting their papers and reading them later, I noticed Jeff's students employed the following Thick question starters:

- Do you think . . . ?

- What do you think . . . ?

- How do you think . . . ?

But the vast majority of the questions were of the Thickest variety. These seventh and eighth graders jumped at the opportunity to be demanding readers and challenge the author's decisions. What the following questions to the author show is that every one of these kids has crossed over the invisible but very real boundary line separating reader and writer. They are insiders now, and I have no doubt they will remain so from this day forward.

- Ryan: "Did you include an intense event in the story in order for Mia to experience a world without color? Did you feel that it was necessary for this to happen in Mia's life for her to grow as a person?"

- Madeline M.: "Why did you decide Mia was going to isolate herself from loved ones when she discovered her synesthesia?"

- Madison: "Would Mia have been better off telling the truth back in second grade?"

- Marcelle: "Reflecting on the whole book, have you been in, or known someone in, similar situations as Mia? How do you know about those situations?"

- Emma: "Why do you think death is such a strong theme for young adult books?"

- Alexa, who studied the book's cover, asked: "Why did you make Mango not lifelike on the cover? Is it a sign that he will die later in the book?"

What truly impressed me about this class was how the students independently generated Thickest questions on their *first attempt,* with very little instruction. They quickly understood the reader's role in cooperating with the author to make meaning. Some of their questions showed a pointed curiosity; others were more critically dubious. But all were polite, respectful, and genuinely interested in learning more from the author. Jeff's class was able to ask Thickest type questions without any teacher prompts. They invented their own question starters, and their list has become an outstanding resource for us to use with our students (see box on next page).

Student-Generated Type III Question Starters

What was the point . . .	Can you explain why you . . . .
What was your point . . .	What was the purpose of . . .
Why did you decide to . . .	Was there a reason you . . .
Why did you make . . .	What's with . . .
Why did you choose . . .	When you were writing this book . . .

Sharing With the Author

To help Jeff out, I typed up students' questions and e-mailed them back to him. He scored them using the three-point system and then clustered them into 18 subtopics for the author of the novel. The clustering took some time, but Jeff felt it was worthwhile to narrow the number of questions. Jeff wanted to send the questions to the author. By reducing the sheer volume, he increased the chances of the author replying. Smart.

Wendy Mass is one of those authors I greatly admire who actually wants to hear from her readers. On her Web site, she lists her e-mail address and encourages students to contact her. Jeff e-mailed the questions to her, and sure enough, Wendy responded:

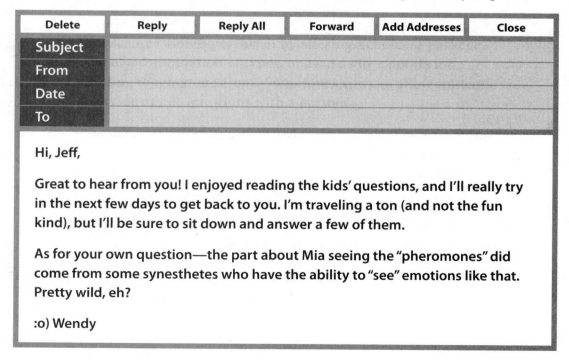

Delete	Reply	Reply All	Forward	Add Addresses	Close

Subject	
From	
Date	
To	

Hi, Jeff,

Great to hear from you! I enjoyed reading the kids' questions, and I'll really try in the next few days to get back to you. I'm traveling a ton (and not the fun kind), but I'll be sure to sit down and answer a few of them.

As for your own question—the part about Mia seeing the "pheromones" did come from some synesthetes who have the ability to "see" emotions like that. Pretty wild, eh?

:o) Wendy

As promised, she responded to all of the question clusters!

| Delete | Reply | Reply All | Forward | Add Addresses | Close |

Subject	
From	
Date	
To	

Hi, Jeff,

I was just thinking about how I needed to get back to you, so thanks for the reminder. And thanks to your students for all the great questions—they really show how closely they read the book.

1. Why did you feel compelled to write a book about synesthesia? Do you know someone who has it?

I didn't know anyone who had it in the beginning, but now I know a lot of people. I just thought it was a really interesting topic that I hadn't seen in fiction before. I always like to write about topics that interest me, figuring they might interest other people, too.

2. Did you include an intense (traumatic) event in the story in order for Mia to experience a world without color? Was this necessary for her to grow as a person?

Yes, I think so. But Mango dying wasn't just a device for her to lose her synesthesia and gain perspective on her life; it was also to try to let the reader know what it can feel like to lose a pet and how it's possible to heal from it, in case they are faced with it themselves.

3. Why did you decide Mia was going to isolate herself from loved ones when she discovered her synesthesia?

I needed to show her struggle with it. The whole thing was essentially the struggle we all go through, especially at that age, of wanting to fit in, but wanting to feel different, too. And sometimes we feel better than everyone else, and I wanted to show how that is kind of destructive.

4. Did you relate to anyone you know, or yourself, when you created some of the characters?

Not the characters so much, but some of the smaller details—the piece of the moon was from my own childhood, as was the friendship bracelets. The baskets marked *Healthy* and *Sick* (or something like that!) was from a friend of mine who actually had a teacher who did that.

5. Why did you make Mia's reaction to Mango's death so strong? Why do that to Mia when she already had such a big problem in her life?

See question 2.

6. Why did you make Mango not lifelike on the cover? Is it a sign that he will die later in the book?

I have no say in the cover, but yes, they did that to show it was the "space" of Mango left behind.

7. What was the point of Roger's character? Was it just to add confusion to Mia's life, or did he serve another purpose?

It helps to introduce a character in a book who hasn't known the main character before. It gives you more opportunities for storytelling. Plus, he was the only one she knew who had lost a pet.

8. Why did you make Adam seem different when Mia meets him in person compared to how he was in the e-mails?

He always was kind of jerky, so willing to lie to his parents, that sort of thing. Just insensitive when Mango died. I think he'll outgrow that stuff though.

9. Why did Billy's mom suddenly have a drastic change of attitude at the end?

I think she finally believed it was real.

10. Why did you make Beth sound like one of the bad guys at the beginning, but in the middle and end her personality changed to be a caring sister?

She wasn't the bad guy, only being herself, which was a pretty self-centered girl. By the end, she and the whole family had been through a lot, so it was natural to me that she'd change and grow, too.

11. Why did you decide to make Mia's parents opposite personalities?

Many couples I know have different personalities—they balance each other out, provide the things they don't have themselves.

12. What was the purpose of having Jenna's dad start dating a girl Jenna didn't like, instead of someone she likes?

So that Jenna would have difficult things going on, too.

13. When you were writing the book, why did you think that the acupuncture sessions served as an important part of the story? Was the effect on Mia based on actual research?

It showed that she was starting to let it get out of control. And yes, a synesthete shared her experience with me and that's what I based it on.

14. Why do you think death is such a strong theme for young adult books?

Because it's something we all fear, and at that age we're only just starting to face that we might not be immortal.

Of course, Jeff printed her answers and gave each student a copy. I was invited back to sit in on the class's reaction to her reply. The kids were ecstatic. They felt honored that a famous author respected them enough to take time to actually write back. And even though they had moved on to the next assigned novel, they easily recalled even the smallest details of her book as they engaged in a spirited conversation.

While it is not necessary or even possible to routinely send students' Type III Questions to the author, you can see the immense advantages of doing so. Realistically, though, if you pull it off once a semester, your students will benefit. For more logistical advice, such as what to do if the author you've assigned is very famous and therefore very busy, or worse, if your author is deceased, see my first book, *Reading Response That Really Matters*.

Reality Check: Questioning in a Lower-Powered Class

The students in Jeff's Book Club course obviously were very academically motivated and highly skilled—an exceptional class that produced exceptional results. But what about higher-level question-asking in a more typical middle school class? Can learners at grade-level ability, or even below, pull off Type III Questions? Of course they can. We just need to provide the proper support. It usually takes them awhile longer to get to the third level, but all learners can get there, especially with solid teaching. I recommend these instructional approaches:

1. **Prime your students for higher-level, critical-thinking questions by constantly referring to the author by name. This plants the seed for lowering the barrier between reader and writer, and opens the door to direct question-asking.**

2. **Teach Type III Questions at the top of a question pyramid rather than in isolation. Refer back to earlier questioning activities, such as Thin and Thick questions, QtA questions, or Sidekick questions (see page 62).**

3. **Model Type III Questions during your instruction. Do it in a natural manner, showing that you cannot help but ask questions that challenge the author.**

4. **Provide students with question starter prompts to guide them into different levels of questioning. Design your own, or feel free to use Jeff's student-generated starters (see page 115). Be sure to promote any new ones your students develop.**

Middle School U.S. History Students Ask Type IIIs

I have used the Three Types of Questions with students at every level. When my regular eighth-grade U.S. History class studied the 1692 Salem Witch Trials, I used the three question types to support their reading. My students realized that our textbook was missing some important information. For example, Adriana asked these questions of the course textbook authors:

> "Even though it [the chapter] was good, it really didn't have enough information for our whole class. Why didn't you tell us more about [the trials]? We needed to go through a lot of [other] sources to get all the information we needed. We had to watch a movie, read theories, search the Internet, and much more. It was REALLY hard to find the info you didn't describe. Why did you make us work so hard?"

Of course, no textbook is responsible for providing *all* the accumulated information on a topic; textbooks can only survey a topic, not go into complete detail. But the students learned an important lesson: Don't rely on any one source, even the course text, for learning about history. There is usually more to the story, and it's up to us to find out. Adrianna's polite but frustrated questioning puts her in a challenging stance—right where a history student belongs. In the seminal *Understanding by Design* (2004), Grant Wiggins and Jay McTighe list "author intent, style, and bias" as critical things to look for when assessing insightful student responses. This is exactly what the class was doing.

So, clearly, typical middle graders are capable of posing more demanding questions to the author. I see no reason to wait until high school to teach them this advanced level. Of course, their developmental levels will vary, so it's up to us to structure it appropriately and to realize a key component of success is a solid understanding of the information presented by the author.

One more point: Adriana's line, "We had to watch a movie, read theories, search the Internet, and much more," is very telling. Sure, she complained about doing all the extra work, but she also demonstrates a key component to questioning: Without access to the supplemental resources, she and her classmates may not have been able to identify the shortcomings of the text. This leads us to the next issue: the role of prior knowledge.

Background Knowledge and Questioning

When an 11th grader can ask Edgar Allan Poe, "Do you believe that the death of a beautiful woman is the most tragic thing you can come up with in a poem?" that student is drawing from prior knowledge of what constitutes tragedy. Critical reading relies on actively accessing relevant prior knowledge at the appropriate time. To become aware of what the text is missing, the reader must know enough about the topic to recognize a gap. To realize the author is expressing a point of view, the reader must be aware of potential opposing viewpoints. To be able to judge an author's writing, the reader must have some previous experience in assessing and evaluating written work. In their seminal book *Strategies That Work* (2000), Stephanie Harvey and Anne Goudvis state "… good questions spring from background knowledge . . . . It's tough to ask a substantive question about something we know or care little about." I know this to be true for myself; I cannot articulately comment on or critique something that I don't know much about. And conversely, the more I know about something, the more questions I have about it. Knowledge seeks more knowledge. And not only for higher-level questions; all questions require some background knowledge.

A.V. Ciardiello writes, "Students need background knowledge to enable them to detect anomalies and develop an awareness of puzzling learning experiences . . . . Students' prior knowledge enabled them to detect anomalies as *threats* to their original preconceptions. (2007) They need well-developed frameworks on the topic . . . ." So, if questioning is connected to background knowledge—as I and the above teachers contend—and some of our students have what Ciardiello terms "limited versus adequate" stores of knowledge, we'd better to something about it.

"Pack the House" with Essential Background Information

I believe the answer is to fill up our student's repositories of knowledge, or "prime their minds," in the words Rick Wormeli, with multimodal classroom experiences. According to teacher-author Jeffery Wilhelm (2007), 50 percent of reading comprehension is based on the reader's prior knowledge. Wow. Now that's enough to get my attention as a teacher. And even if it's only, say 37%, that's still very important.

Why multimodal experiences? In *Building Background Knowledge for Academic Achievement* (2004), Robert Marzano tells us that "Memories are bi-modal: linguistic and nonlinguistic packets." This comes as no surprise to teachers; we know our students' brains process information in different modes, and that an overreliance on the book-oriented mode does not serve all our learners well. Therefore, for prereading, I like to use an abundance of mixed-media events in the classroom to fill the gap between students' direct knowledge and what the learning assignment requires. Let's bring in some nonlinguistic along with the linguistic! Here are useful examples:

- mini-lectures from the teacher

- mini-lectures accompanied by a computer slide show with pictures (using Powerpoint or Mac's Keynote)

- teacher story/personal narrative about the topic

- whole-class conversation

- brief introduction to key concepts by assigning a supplemental reading assignment

- videotape or DVD

- Web-based video clip from commercial streaming site (e.g., unitedstreaming.com, learn360.com, brainpop.com)

- Web site shown to whole class via a computer projector or interactive white board that introduces or relates to the topic

- music played for the class that connects, introduces, or relates to the topic.

- a volunteer acts out, role-plays, or mimes some aspect of the topic

- students illustrate what they already know using an Open Mind or SnapShots activity for examples, visit larrylewin.com/books/extraresources/questioningstrategies.html)

I am not advocating that we employ *all* of the above, nor I am suggesting that anything less than an onslaught of these kinds of events is inadequate. It's just that the more we "pack the house" with information, the better off our students will be. Marzano refers to the research of Graham Nuthall, who found that "students require about four exposures to information to adequately integrate it into their background knowledge." So, the more the better. Let's invest in their success by generously funding their deposits of background information. The more they know, the easier they can ask for more.

Dialectical Notebooks

Here is an activity designed by the College Board called Dialectical Notebooks. It offers a nice variation on the Three Types of Questions activity. Students divide a piece of paper into two columns: a text column and a response column. In the first column, students record what they consider to be the major points of a particular text. Students record their personal reactions to the text—comments, questions, ideas—in the second column.

The College Board recommends that students use symbols to indicate their responses in the second column, which is a great idea (see Figure 4.2). Both you and your students can invent additional symbol codes as you explore this activity. The goal, as always, is to foster student self-monitoring of reading to support improved comprehension. And while this particular activity was designed to support Advanced Placement students, it works for learners at all levels.

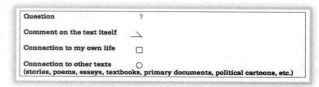

Figure 4.2 Symbols for question types used by the College Board

I like this activity because it broadens students' responses to a reading assignment from just asking questions to commenting on the text and making connections to their personal experience and other texts. It also fosters the worthwhile skill of summarization, helps students to agree on the facts, and lets the teacher know that the students have all read the same text.

For our purposes, we can further subdivide the question category into three types of questions and label them T I, T II, and T III.

- **T I question** a review question to help me remember key information (literal level)

- **T II question** a more open-ended question that helps me think more deeply about the information (interpretative/inferential level)

- **T III question** a probing question about the author's purpose and intention (evaluative level)

Here are some examples from a science textbook chapter that use the codes:

1. Why do human genes vary?
   (T I: the answer is right there in the text)

2. Do human genes vary by racial groups?
   (T II: the answer is not in the text)

3. Does the author think genome mapping has any unforeseen problems?
(T III: the question probes the author's implicit point of view)

Modifications to Consider

While we can always try a new activity and use it as is, we can often adapt it and make it better for our students. Here are some modifications that come to mind for Dialectical Notebooks:

MODIFICATIONS FOR DIALECTICAL NOTEBOOKS

1. Instead of using notebooks, students could write their responses on sticky notes and place them onto the text. They could code their responses by using the same symbols (see box above) in the corner of a sticky note before writing their response on the note.

2. Speaking of sticky notes, you could provide four different colors and assign one color for questions, another color for comments, etc.

3. Instead of starting with the four categories in the box above, narrow student responses to just one or two to ease them into this new activity.

4. Instead of using the four categories, use only the question category subdivided into Type I, Type II, and Type III by assigning a color sticky note for each. Ask students, "Can anyone invent symbols for these three types of questions?"

5. Use the two categories recommended by Linda Christensen (2000): "Observations/Quotes," where readers record notes from the reading, and "Reactions/Reflections" where readers jot down their own thoughts and questions.

6. In place of spiral notebooks, distribute college exam blue books to students. While many teachers have a negative association with blue books, our students do not. In fact, they like them because they are shorter and thinner, and therefore less intimidating than spirals.

7. Anything else you can dream up to support your students.

Summary

Advanced-level questioning relies on a foundation of earlier question-asking activities. The ones presented in this last chapter build upon those in the first three chapters. The Three Types of Questions activity advances a reader's questioning to the highest level of thinking: critiquing the author. But for students to be able to take this stance, they first need to be comfortable generating questions while reading. Thus, Type I questions refer to literal-level comprehension-checking questions, Type IIs require digging deeper into the text, and Type IIIs take on a skeptical attitude to challenge the author. Dialectical Notebooks foster a similar complexity in readers' responses, by offering a choice of questioning, commenting, and making connections.

This chapter also addressed a key prerequisite for advanced questioning: possessing the essential background knowledge of the topic. Many researchers, and practitioners alike, recognize and embrace the role prior knowledge plays in supporting comprehension in general and questioning in particular. I shared a menu of multimodal classroom activities designed to get all readers up to speed so they can discern what is working and not working for them.

Conclusion

Throughout this book, you no doubt picked up on my great enjoyment with students behaving untraditionally in the classroom. When kids are able to act as mature, responsible, engaged learners, I like my job. When they are willing and able to bump up their thinking and become questioning, critiquing, demanding thinkers, I am pleased to be present in school with them. When they read with interest, enthusiasm, and care, I am proud be a member of the education community. I became a teacher 35 years ago to help move students from the traditional, passive, I'm-here-because-I-have-to-be attitude to one of: "I'm here, and I am actually enjoying using my brain!"

Like you, I have been fortunate over the years to work with students who come to class already functioning at a high level of thinking and with above-grade-level skills in reading. Likewise, we all experience working with kids who have trouble reading and thinking simultaneously, and therefore are not engaged, inspired, or excited about reading. I wrote this book for them.

Student questioning is not a new idea, for sure, but it is one that too often is overlooked or underutilized. Questioning while reading is essential for the mental engagement that is required for comprehension. Isabel Beck and Margaret McKeown said it best: "Reading and questioning have a *symbiotic relationship*."

I wholeheartedly agree. That is why I've spent my career both creating and collecting question-asking activities that foster better reading and thinking. Take these questioning activities, try them out, reorganize them, and tweak them as needed for your own students. Then, please, somehow find a moment to let me know how they worked out. My e-mail is larry@larrylewin.com, and I promise you that I am the kind of author who responds.

Bibliography

Beck I. L., & McKeown, M. G. (2006). *Improving comprehension with questioning the author: A fresh and expanded view of a powerful approach.* New York: Scholastic.

Beck, I. L., & McKeown, M. G. (1997). *Questioning the author: An approach for enhancing student engagement with text.* Newark, DE: International Reading Association.

Bloom, B. S., Engelhart, M. D., Furst, E. J., Hill, W. H., & Krathwohl, D. R. (1956). *Taxonomy of educational objectives: The classification of educational goals.* New York: Longmans, Green and Company.

Christensen, L. (2000). *Reading, writing, and rising up: Teaching about social justice and the power of the written word,* Milwaukee: Rethinking Schools, Ltd.

Carnine, D. (2006). *World history: Ancient civilizations.* Geneva, IL: McDougal Littell.

Ciardiello, A. V. (2007). *Puzzle them first: Motivating adolescent readers with question-finding.* Newark, DE: International Reading Association.

Daniels, H. (2002). *Literature circles: Voice and choice in book clubs and reading groups.* Portland, ME: Stenhouse.

Davey, B. (1983). Think aloud: Modeling the cognitive processes of reading comprehension. *Journal of Reading,* 27, 44–47.

Durkin, D. (1978-79). What classroom observations reveal about reading comprehension instruction. *Reading Research Quarterly,* 14, 481–533.

Harvey S. & Goudvis, A. (2000). *Strategies that work.* Portland, ME: Stenhouse.

Heacox, D. (2002). *Differentiating the regular classroom: How to read and teach all learners, Grades 3–12.* Minneapolis: Free Spirit Publishing.

Ihimaera, W. (1987). *The whale rider.* New York: Harcourt.

Jensen, E. BrighterBrain® Bulletin. Retrieved May 1, 2008.

Kagan, S. (1994). *Cooperative learning.* San Clemente, CA: Resources for Teachers.

Kohn, Alfie. (2004). PHI DELTA KAPPAN, November 2004. Available online at http://www.alfiekohn.org/teaching/challenging.htm

Lamb, A., & Johnson, L. (2003). Literary criticism. Retrieved from: http://42explore.com/litcrit.htm

Lewin, L. (2006). *Reading response that really matters to middle schoolers.* New York: Scholastic.

Lexile Analyzer, MetaMetrics. Retrieved April 2, 2008, from http://www.lexile.com/DesktopDefault.aspx?view=ed&tabindex=2&tabid=16&tabpageid=335

Lovgren, S. (2006). Can cell-phone recycling help African gorillas? National Geographic News. Retrieved from http://news.nationalgeographic.com/news/pf/82412963.html

Marzano, R. (2004). *Building background knowledge for academic achievement.* Alexandria, VA: ASCD.

Mass, W. (2003). *A mango-shaped space.* New York: Little, Brown and Co.

McKeown, M. G., Beck, I. L., & Worthy, M. J. (1993). Grappling with text ideas: Questioning the author. *The Reading Teacher,* 47, 560–566.

Milne, H. (2000). *Human body systems: Science technology concepts for middle schools.* Washington DC: Smithsonian/The National Academics, National Science Resources Center.

National Assessment of Educational Progress (2007). What does the NAEP reading assessment measure? Retrieved from http://nces.ed.gov/nationsreportcard/reading/whatmeasure.asp

The National Teaching and Learning Forum (2008). Classroom assessment techniques–CATs. Retrieved from http://www.ntlf.com/html/lib/bib/assess.htm

Palinscar, A.S. & and Brown, A. (1984). Reciprocal teaching of comprehension-fostering and comprehension-monitoring activities. *Cognition and Instruction,* Vol. 1, No. 2, 117–75.

Pashler H., et al. (2007). Enhancing learning and retarding forgetting: Choices and consequences. *Psychonomic Bulletin Review.* 14(2):187–93.

Pashler H., et al. (2005). When does feedback facilitate learning of words? 31(1): 3–8. *Journal of Experimental Psychology: Learning, Memory, and Cognition*

Paulsen, G. (1990). *Woodsong.* New York: Simon & Schuster Children's Publishing.

Prelutsky, J., (Ed.). (2003). *Read-aloud rhymes for the very young.* Minneapolis: Fairview Press.

Probst, R. E. (1987). Transactional theory in the teaching of literature. Urbana IL: ERIC Clearinghouse on Reading and Communication Skills. ERIC Document Reproduction Services No. ED284274

Poe, E. A. (1846). The philosophy of composition. Retrieved from http://xroads.virginia.edu/~HYPER/poe/composition.html

Questioning the author in strategies for reading comprehension. Retrieved 4/4/08, fromhttp://curry.edschool.virginia.edu/go/readquest/strat/qta.html.

Rabinowitz, Y.S., & Smith, S.G. (1998). *Authorizing readers: Resistance and respect in the teaching of literature.* New York: Teachers College Press.

Raphael, T., Highfield, K., & Au, K. (2006). *QAR Now: A powerful and practical framework that develops comprehension and higher-level thinking in all students.* New York: Scholastic.

Rosenblatt, L. (1986). The aesthetic transaction. *Journal of Aesthetic Education,* 20, No. 4.

Scardamalia, M., & Bereiter, C. (1992). Text-based and knowledge-based questioning by children. *Cognition and Instruction,* 9(3), 177–199 (2007)

Simon, S., Howe, L., & Kirshchenbaum, H. (1972). *Values clarification.* New York: Hart Publishing Co.

Tanaka, S. (1999). *Secrets of the mummies.* New York: Hyperion.

UCLA chemist provides insights into science icon: Chemistry's periodic table (2006). Retrieved from http://www.brightsurf.com/news/headlines/27641/ULCA_chemist_provides_insights_into_science_icon_Chemistrys_periodic_table.html

Wilhelm, J. (2007). *Engaging readers & writers with inquiry: Promoting deep understandings in language arts and the content areas with guiding questions.* New York: Scholastic.

Wilhelm, J. (2004). *Reading is seeing.* New York: Scholastic.

Wormeli, R. (2006). *Fair isn't always equal: Assessing and grading in the differentiated classroom.* Portland, ME: Stenhouse.

Yopp-Edwards, R. (2003) The reading connection in *Reading Educators Guild Newsletter,* Volume 32, Issue 2, March/April. Retrieved from http://www.readingeducatorsguild.org/newsletters/news3202.htm.